WRONGFULLY CONVICTED

The Innocent in Canada

PETER BOER

QUAGMIRE
PRESS

© 2007 Quagmire Press Ltd.
First printed in 2007 10 9 8 7 6 5 4 3 2 1
Printed in Canada

The Publisher: Quagmire Press Ltd.
Website: www.quagmirepress.com

Library and Archives Canada Cataloguing in Publication

Boer, Peter, 1977–
Wrongfully convicted : the innocent in Canada / by Peter Boer.

Includes bibliographical references.
ISBN-10: 0-978340-91-4
ISBN-13: 978-0-978340-91-9

1. Judicial error—Canada. I. Title.

KE9440.B64 2007   347.71'012   C2007-905261-4   KF9756.B64 2007

Project Director: Lisa Wojna
Project Editor: Tara Woloschuk
Production: Jodene Draven
Cover Image: Courtesy of Photos.com / © 2007 JupiterImages Corporation

PC: P5

Contents

Dedication

To Derek, for your friendship and support

Acknowledgements

This book would not have been possible without the ongoing support of Lisa Wojna of Quagmire Press. To Tara Woloschuk for her seamless and dedicated editing to help tell these stories. To my friends for their continuing support in my endeavours— thank you. And to my colleagues of the press who have shaken these stories out of the bushes. The world needs more journalists like you.

Introduction

The existence of our criminal justice system is proof that people make mistakes. The stories in this book are proof that the people responsible for administering our justice system are also fallible.

I think everyone has found themselves in a situation where someone has accused them of doing something they haven't done. Those situations, usually social in nature, do not carry particularly onerous consequences.

But imagine yourself locked in a jail cell for 23 hours a day, housed with murderers, sexual predators and other life-long criminals, convicted of a particularly brutal crime that you absolutely know you did not commit. Imagine the drowning sensation that comes with knowing that an entire system is against you, the frustration of continually having your story rebuffed or the despair of realizing that few people, if any, believe you.

That's what the six men whose stories are told in this book were forced to endure. From David Milgaard, who spent more than two decades behind bars, to Wilbert Coffin, who died at the end of the hangman's noose, each of these men suffered at the hands of a justice system that in almost every case desperately needed to convict someone to quell public fear and restore trust in the judicial system.

We depend on our police to keep our communities safe by enforcing the laws enacted by our government. We depend on our judges and Crown prosecutors to put those who break our laws in jail. And we depend on our jailers to make sure that criminals' sentences are carried out. Our general sense of well-being stems from our belief that all these people are looking out for our best interests by properly trying and punishing the guilty.

This book is not intended as an assault on the criminal justice system in Canada. In fact, I strongly believe in the way our justice system works. Having worked as a court and crime reporter, I have seen the players in the system first-hand as they go about their work, and I believe not just in the work they do, but in how they do it. They are, as one police officer once told me, the blue band separating the two-thirds of us from the one-third who would harm us.

It's important to remember, however, that the people who work as our police officers, prosecutors and judges are, like those they put in prison, human beings who can make mistakes. And sometimes those mistakes have grave consequences.

Speaking from experience, I can state unequivocally that it is exceedingly rare for an innocent person to be charged with a crime and brought before the courts. When criminals are acquitted at trial, it is often because the evidence tendered does not support their conviction—hence, why a person is found "not guilty" of a charge instead of "innocent." Being innocent implies a total absence of involvement in a crime. A verdict of not guilty implies only that there isn't sufficient evidence to confirm a person's responsibility for a crime.

But I believe that the men described in this book are innocent. They are in no way responsible for the crimes of which they were wrongfully convicted. They are victims of police tunnel vision, shifting loyalties, errors of law and simple human frailty.

Tunnel vision is one of the dangers of police work. Sometimes a suspect seems to fit a particular crime so perfectly that investigators fail to consider pursuing leads that may point away from that person. Steven Truscott, whose appeal of his 1959 conviction of the rape and murder of Lynne Harper is currently before the Ontario Court of Appeal, was a victim of police tunnel vision because he openly admitted to being with Harper on the night she died. The then 14-year-old Clinton, Ontario, resident told everyone who asked that he had given 12-year-old Harper a ride on his bike down to the highway outside of town. There is no evidence that the Ontario Provincial Police officer who investigated the murder considered anyone else as a suspect, even though two of Truscott's friends told the courts they saw Truscott giving Harper a ride in the direction of the highway and then saw him return alone.

Guy Paul Morin was also a victim of police tunnel vision. The young man was accused and convicted of murdering Christine Jessop, his next-door neighbour. The police had no viable suspects until Jessop's mother remarked to investigators that Morin was "weird." What followed was an investigation focused only on Morin, even though the police were made aware of several other suspects in the area who could have been responsible for Jessop's death.

If the police accused me of murder, and my closest friends knew that I was not responsible for it, I would hope they would have the intestinal fortitude to tell the police the truth. In the case of David Milgaard, the shifting loyalties of his so-called friends were directly responsible for landing the teenager in jail for the rape and murder of nursing student Gail Miller in 1969. One of his companions, who had been with him on the morning of the crime, turned the Saskatchewan teen in to the police for a $2,000 reward even though he knew Milgaard wasn't responsible. Two other friends later crumbled under brutal police questioning, inventing stories that implicated Milgaard in Miller's death. The police took the young adults at their word even though convicted sex offender Larry Fisher, since convicted of the crime, lived in the area.

Donald Marshall Junior was also a victim of his friends' lies when he was convicted of murdering Sandy Seale in Sydney,

Nova Scotia, in 1971. Marshall was with Seale when Seale was stabbed to death and was even injured in the attack, but two teens who knew Marshall testified that they saw him stab Seale. Both would later admit they hadn't been anywhere near the crime scene at the time of the attack, but had lied under police pressure to make their stories fit with the police's theory of the crime.

Our laws are only as strong as the people charged with interpreting them, and no one knows that better than Thomas Sophonow. The Vancouver man, convicted of killing restaurant waitress Barbara Stoppel in Winnipeg in 1981, went through three separate trials, one of which resulted in a hung jury and the remaining two in guilty verdicts. Twice the Manitoba Court of Appeal ordered a new trial or overturned the verdict. After overturning the verdict of his third trial, the court ordered that Sophonow would not face a fourth trial. His trials were fraught with inappropriate conduct on the part of the judges who over-saw the case, who either misinterpreted the body of case law applicable to the trial, allowed the Crown to engage in question-able tactics with respect to witnesses, disallowed testimony from potentially helpful witnesses for the defence or filled the jury's charge with so much personal opinion that the jury couldn't help but be influenced in evaluating the case.

Each case in this book is dominated by one enduring theme—simple human frailty. Wilbert Coffin, convicted of the murder of three American hunters in Québec's Gaspé region in 1953, fell victim to an inept defence attorney who, after declaring to the press he would call no fewer than 85 witnesses to the stand in Coffin's defence, didn't present a single shred of evidence when his turn came. The jury, 12 simple townsfolk who were sitting and waiting for Coffin to explain his side of the story, never heard from the man and, based on the evidence with which they were supplied, however faulty it might have been, voted to convict the Anglican prospector. Of the cases described in this book, Coffin's is one that will never be definitively rebutted; the World War II veteran was sentenced to death and executed by hanging in 1956, all the while declaring his innocence.

Our justice system can make mistakes, but when review-ing these six cases, it seems almost unfathomable that so many different people with different responsibilities could have made so many mistakes, all contributing to the accused's conviction.

Part of the problem is with the system itself. Once a per-son is convicted of a crime, he or she is assumed to be guilty. A prison guard I once interviewed for a story highlighted this attitude when she said, "We're not the judge. If they say 'I'm innocent,' it's not my issue. I'm just here to help you do your time." There are also few courses of action available for people who maintain they have been wrongfully convicted and want to appeal the decision.

Anyone convicted of a crime in Canada, unless he or she is found to be a dangerous offender, is eligible for parole after serving a minimum prison term. But a key factor in earning that parole is admitting one's guilt and demonstrating some insight into how one's behaviours have affected others. It's a Catch-22 for people wrongfully convicted of a crime. They can't earn parole unless they admit they are guilty, but how can they admit to committing a crime they are innocent of?

There is a section 690 appeal under the Criminal Code, which asks the federal minister of justice to review a conviction and order an appropriate remedy if there are suspicions the conviction might be wrongful. The biggest problem, however, is politics. A political figure can use his or her political advantage either for or against the convict. Kim Campbell declined David Milgaard's first section 690 appeal. It was Prime Minister Brian Mulroney who eventually pressured Campbell into ordering the Supreme Court's review of Milgaard's conviction.

The judicial and executive branches of government are separate for a reason—so neither can abuse the other with its authority. Critics have lobbied for an independent body of some sort apart from the government that would review the cases of suspected wrongfully convicted men and women. After researching the content for this book, I can't help but agree. People married to the system are often unable to see its flaws. A case should be decided on its own merits.

Almost every case described in this book proves the effectiveness of another element of our society—the free press. Dedicated journalists and reporters took the time to ask the questions that others were too afraid to and get the answers. Respected reporters such as Kirk Makin, Jacques Hébert and

Julian Sher took their investigations one step further and published entire books arguing the cases of those who have been wrongfully convicted. Anyone interested in learning more about each individual case should consult the books listed in the Notes on Sources. Obviously, journalistic objectivity can be set aside when reporters start pursuing causes they believe in strongly. But if it turns out they're right, objectivity doesn't really matter in the end.

The six men whose cases are described in this book are not the only people in Canada every wrongfully convicted of a crime. The stories of James Driskell, Randy Druken, Ron Dalton, Romeo Phillion and Gregory Parsons all deserve to be told too. I encourage you to research their cases as well.

We can continue to uncover the Morins and Sophonows and Truscotts in our justice system and continue to pay out millions of dollars in compensation, but no amount of money can ever truly repay these people for the years of their lives consumed by jail time and public derision. We owe it to them to take a hard look at our justice system and start coming up with solutions and safeguards to ensure no one must again be forced to experience what they did.

Justice, after all, is meaningless if it's wrong.

Chapter One

David Milgaard

Toronto, Ontario
November 8, 1980

In his Zippo lighter, he sees the killer's face
Maybe it's someone standing in a killer's place
Twenty years for nothing, well that's nothing new
Besides, no one's interested in something you didn't do
— *Wheat Kings* by the Tragically Hip

There was freedom in Canada's largest city. Of the millions of people living in Toronto, few could pick out a single face from the masses that walked the streets and packed the subway. Size brings anonymity, and that's what David McAdam was counting on.

His picture had been splashed all over the country, yet McAdam was just another face in the millions who commuted to work every day. This anonymous city, for all its drudgery, felt like heaven. In Toronto he was free to do as he wished, to live life as he chose without impediment, without restraint. He could leave his room any time he wanted and stay out as late as he felt like.

He didn't have a job anymore. When he first arrived in Toronto, he'd found work selling encyclopedias but eventually lost that job. He was back to his old ways now, panhandling for money, asking strangers on the street for any spare change they may have. Sometimes he worked as a day labourer. It barely made him enough money to survive, but he required so little. All he needed was a roof over his head and a door that wasn't locked 24 hours a day, 7 days a week.

He knew he was running on borrowed time, knew that his run from the law couldn't last forever, but he was determined to make the most of it. All that was left for him outside Toronto was a lifetime of confinement and abuse, locked behind a prison wall for a crime he maintained he didn't commit. It didn't matter anymore that no one seemed to care. It didn't matter that his flight only made his situation look worse than it really was. All McAdam had was today. Tomorrow might never come.

He even had a girlfriend. He had met Rhonda outside a record store, and the two had quickly become close. They spent their time wandering the city, staking out spots to panhandle a bit more. Eventually, he told her his secret, and she didn't run away. She believed him. And people like that were few in McAdam's life. Only his family believed his side of the story, and he hadn't spoken with them since the day he had run away.

It had been strangely easy. He had known that his escort that day trusted him not to run, but in a moment of impulse, McAdam just couldn't help himself. Left alone with his sister while playing pool during a family visit, McAdam had run out the door the second his escort had disappeared. What followed was inevitable—press releases, news stories, warnings about how he was dangerous. He wasn't dangerous, but no one else knew it. No one else believed it. And he didn't care how guilty running made him look. The alternative was akin to a slow suicide, a fate he couldn't change anymore. If he hadn't run, he would simply have had to resign himself to a living hell.

Then came that day in November when it all fell apart. He didn't know he was being watched, didn't know the police were waiting for him until it was too late. He ran when he saw the shirts coming for him, churning his legs as fast he could to stay just out of their reach. He would never be able to get away, he knew, but he couldn't just surrender. He couldn't give up without trying.

Suddenly there was a crack he barely heard and something smacked him in the rear end, sending him crashing to the pavement. Before he could move, rough hands were on him, restraining him. He could feel a stinging sensation in his buttocks and knew with woeful certainty that his brief moment of freedom was over.

The story made headlines across Canada—David Milgaard, convicted in 1970 of savagely raping and murdering Gail

Miller in Saskatoon, was back in custody after being on the lam for 76 days. He'd been chased down by the police and shot in the rear as he ran away. He'd been living in Toronto under the assumed name of David McAdam.

In 1980 no one cared that Milgaard might be innocent. By the end of the decade, that had changed.

As Canadian cities go, Saskatoon, Saskatchewan, was small in 1969, and murder was a rare event.

So when the police received a report that a child had found a body in the snow on her way to school on January 31, 1969, the response was immediate. Numerous police cruisers descended on the alleyway in the Pleasant Hill district and cordoned off the area. What the investigators saw in the snow at their feet was enough to turn the strongest stomach.

The young woman was dead and had been for a little while. Her dress and underwear had been pushed down to her ankles, and her right boot was missing. When they finally turned her over, the police discovered two things: who she was and how she died.

The nametag on her dress read G. Miller and had been issued by the Saskatoon Institute of Applied Arts and Sciences. By noon, the police had positively identified the victim as Gail Miller, 20, of Laura, Saskatchewan. The nursing assistant had been due at work at the Saskatoon City Hospital that morning and never showed up. She lived only a few blocks from where her body was found and typically caught the bus to work in the mornings.

The cause of death was easily inferred from the condition of the body. Miller's throat, chest and back were littered with angry red wounds, obviously the work of a knife. The state of her dress and panties implied that she'd likely been raped.

The snow around her body had been kicked and stomped on, but there were no tire marks to be found. A search of the area turned up a few clues, but none would help in tracking down her killer. One officer found the blade of a bloodstained kitchen paring knife that was later confirmed to be the murder weapon, but there were no fingerprints on it or the handle, which was found later. One officer isolated two yellowish clumps of frozen snow that investigators thought might be semen stains, but with no suspect to test the sample against, they were practically useless. The police found Miller's purse in a nearby garbage can. There was no money in it and no fingerprints that could be lifted. Miller had not led a high-risk lifestyle, had no enemies or jilted lovers. She had been a regular person on her way to her job to help people, when she'd been attacked.

The police started canvassing the neighbourhood and questioned everyone who could have seen something, but no one had. Some of the people at Miller's apartment building confirmed they had seen her at 6:45 AM that morning. Her body had been found shortly after 8:00 AM, meaning she had not been dead for long by the time she was found. No one else had any information to offer. The police were staring at a dead end scarcely after they had begun looking.

An autopsy confirmed the brutality of the slaying. Dr. Harry Emerson told the police that Miller had been stabbed almost 30 times. Of the wounds he counted, 15 were superficial slash marks to the upper torso, differing in length and depth. The remaining 12 were scattered across her front, back, collarbone and side. Two of the stab wounds had punctured her right lung, and they were identified as the cause of death. The autopsy also confirmed the presence of semen in Miller's vagina, and the motility of the sperm indicated that intercourse had occurred no more than 12 hours before death. Emerson estimated Miller had been dead for roughly one hour before she was found, meaning her death had likely occurred sometime around 7:30 that morning.

When the news got out, the effect on the public was intense. Not only was the population of Saskatoon shocked by the murder, but the women in the city were suddenly jolted into action. Two women called in to report that they had been raped in the same area of the city in which Miller's body was found. In both cases, the women had been attacked from behind, threatened with a knife, dragged into an isolated area such as an alley and raped.

With their leads running out and no suspects on which to focus, the police put out a call to the general public, offering a $2,000 reward for any information that would lead to the arrest of Miller's killer. The result was immediate as the phones at the local detachment started ringing off the hook. Almost every tip called in amounted to nothing, but the investigators were obliged to check out each one. There was mounting public pressure on the police to solve the crime and find the killer.

On March 2, 1969, Albert "Shorty" Cadrain walked into the station to report that he knew who the killer was.

~

David Milgaard was a hippy.

He had long hair, used recreational drugs and had a relaxed attitude towards sex. His attitude was so relaxed, in fact, that his friends called him Hoppy because of the frequency with which he leapt in and out of girls' beds.

And Milgaard was a little lost in life in 1969. He took each day as it came, but never made much out of it. He lived in Langenburg, Saskatchewan, with his parents and was known as a big prankster. He could be a disagreeable and difficult teen, so much so that he'd spent a few months in a psychiatric hospital. The doctor's released him, saying he was normal, just a little rebellious. He quit school in Grade 9 and spent his time hitch-hiking across the country, panhandling for whatever money he needed to get to his next destination.

It was that lust for adventure and travel that would land Milgaard in jail for the next 23 years.

He was hanging out at a restaurant in Regina on the night of January 30, 1969, when he ran into his friend Ron Wilson. Wilson had just received a 1958 Pontiac from his parents for Christmas and was eager to show it off. The best way to do that, they reasoned, was by taking a road trip to Alberta and seeing just what the car could do.

"It was just kind of a 'take off and see what happens' trip," Milgaard later said. "It was even better than hitchhiking. You didn't have to find a car."

At first, the car couldn't do much. The battery was shot, so the pair stole one from another car and replaced it. Three of the tires were also flat, so they took the car to a garage. They got on the road just after midnight, joined by one of Milgaard's lady friends, a young drug addict by the name of Nichol John, who had quit her waitressing job at a restaurant that night to join them.

They had one stop to make before they headed to Alberta, and that was in Saskatoon. Milgaard wanted to stop in on one of his friends, Shorty Cadrain, and see if he wanted to come along. They rolled into Saskatoon sometime between 5:30 and 6:30 AM, only to discover that Milgaard didn't know how to get to Cadrain's place. They tried asking a woman for directions, but she couldn't help them. After making a quick stop at a local motel to buy a map and ask for directions, they headed back out.

While driving through the city, they pulled down an alley and came across a man who was trying to free his car from the mountains of snow that had accumulated in the city. The trio got out to help the man, whose name was Walter Danchuk, but in the process of doing so, Wilson's car stopped running. Danchuk invited all three of them inside his home to wait for the tow truck. After a quick stop at the garage, they were able to find Cadrain's house, located in Pleasant Hill. Cadrain lived upstairs, while a couple by the name of Larry and Linda Fisher lived in the home's basement.

Cadrain eagerly agreed to join in on the road trip. Before they left, the other three watched as Milgaard changed out of his pants because he had ripped them while trying to free Danchuk's car. They drove all the way to Calgary, stopping along the way, even going so far as to break into a grain elevator at one point.

Shortly after their return to Saskatchewan, the police arrested Cadrain for vagrancy in Regina, for which he spent a week in jail. During that time, investigators asked him if he knew anything about Gail Miller's murder. The young man claimed he didn't know anything.

On March 2, that all changed when Cadrain walked into the police detachment with a story about who might have killed Miller.

~

He hadn't actually seen the murder, Cadrain told the police, but he had seen a few things on his road trip that made him wonder if the killer hadn't been under his nose the whole time.

Cadrain confirmed that when Milgaard, Wilson and John first arrived at his home, Milgaard had changed his pants in full view of everyone. As he did so, Cadrain saw what he was sure was blood on Milgaard's clothes.

Later that night, Cadrain said, as the foursome had sped down the highway to Alberta, he had seen Milgaard grab a cosmetics case and throw it out of the window of the moving car. According to Cadrain, Milgaard had told him when they arrived in Alberta that he was a member of the Mafia and wanted to have Wilson and John killed because "they knew too much."

The part about the Mafia might have been a bit much for investigators, but it was the most substantial lead they had received to date. They went looking for Wilson, but realized they didn't have to go far. He was in jail, serving a prison sentence for theft. Wilson, however, was of little help at first. After questioning him for a while, the police had Wilson sign a statement saying he had seen Milgaard change his pants, but that Milgaard was never out of his sight during the trip and, as far as he knew, never carried a knife.

The police also tracked down John, but she was of no more help than Wilson had been. Her story closely mirrored Wilson's when she insisted she hadn't seen anything strange about Milgaard's behaviour during the trip. With no other options, two officers tracked down Milgaard and spent six hours grilling him about the road trip. David never asked for a lawyer and answered all their questions. He let the two officers inspect his body and search his motel room. They found no scars or wounds on his body and no incriminating evidence in his room.

Yet Milgaard was the only lead the police had, so they were loath to let him go so easily. They started questioning Wilson more frequently, telling the 17-year-old that they had evidence he was lying, that he could also be a prime suspect in the case. They took him to Saskatoon to visit the crime scene and walked him through what they had found. They hooked him up to a lie detector and asked him questions and then told him the machine proved he was lying. They showed him Miller's clothes, an assortment of knives and her wallet, which was found April 4 outside Cadrain's house. At one point, they brought John into the room and interviewed the pair together. The police were relentless in their investigation, almost criminal in their continued harassment of both Wilson and, it later turned out, John. Both were teenagers, drug users, kids who were in over their heads. It was only a matter of time before they cracked.

Piecing together what information the police had shared with him, Wilson changed his story. He told the police about the woman they had stopped to ask for directions who couldn't help them and how he had heard Milgaard call her a "stupid bitch." He said he had seen Milgaard carrying a knife during the drive from Regina to Saskatoon. He said that after the car died outside the Danchuk residence, he and Milgaard had split up and gone in different directions to look for help. When Wilson returned, he had found a hysterical John in the car. Five minutes later, Milgaard had shown up, breathing heavily and saying something about "I fixed her."

Wilson said he had also seen blood on Milgaard's pants. He told the police that John had found a cosmetics case in the car, and when asked about it, Milgaard had grabbed it and thrown it out the window. Wilson said that when the foursome arrived in Calgary, Milgaard had told him he had "hit" or "got" a girl and thrown her purse in a trashcan.

John also withered under the brutality of the investigators' interviewing procedures. They took her to the crime scene, showed her the evidence and briefly locked her up in a cell. Deprived of the drugs she used almost daily, John emerged from the cell and scribbled out a rambling 10-page statement saying she had witnessed Milgaard stab Miller.

"Dave reached into one of his pockets and pulled out the knife. I don't know which pocket he got the knife from. The knife was in his right hand. I don't know if Dave had a hold of this girl or not at this time. All I recall is seeing him stabbing her with the knife."

That Milgaard was left-handed didn't seem to bother investigators. Between Cadrain, Wilson and John, the police now had three witnesses who somehow recited evidence that incriminated Milgaard. In 1969, when there was no such thing as DNA matching, corroborating eyewitness testimony was the best evidence a police officer could hope for.

On May 31, 1969, the police arrested Milgaard in Prince George, BC, where he worked selling magazine subscriptions. He was 17 years old.

~

In 1969, Canada still executed murderers. Fortunately for Milgaard, the charge laid against him didn't warrant such punishment.

Milgaard was officially charged by the police with non-capital murder. At the time, the offence of capital murder was generally reserved for criminals found guilty of killing police officers or prison guards. That fact, however, would prove to be of little consolation to Milgaard. A conviction for non-capital murder automatically required a life sentence with no statutory parole eligibility. If found guilty, he could spend the rest of his natural life behind bars.

Remanded into police custody, Milgaard soon became familiar with the confines of a prison cell. He was allowed out to visit with his lawyer, Calvin Tallis, who had been appointed by Legal Aid. Milgaard's mother, Joyce, also moved to Saskatoon, took a job as a waitress and lived at the local YWCA so she could be closer to her son. No one in the Milgaard family, especially Joyce, believed for a second that David was guilty.

At a speed no longer possible in the Canadian judicial system, Milgaard's preliminary inquiry began on August 18, 1969, less than three months after his arrest. A preliminary inquiry is a pre-trial of sorts in which a judge listens to the Crown's evidence and determines whether or not there is enough information to substantiate the charge laid and warrant a trial. The outcome of the inquiry is seldom in doubt because it is not a proceeding that attributes guilt; the judge need only be satisfied that the Crown has a reasonable chance of proving its case at trial. Defendants are almost always bound over for trial.

The proceedings lasted three weeks, during which time the Crown called 42 witnesses. Unfortunately for Milgaard, there was no such thing in 1969 as a publication ban for a preliminary inquiry, and the media turned up in droves, reporting every detail of the Crown's case. The witnesses for the prosecution performed as expected, with Wilson, John and Cadrain all telling the stories the police had figuratively beaten into them. Cadrain's testimony, however, took a turn for the strange. He told Judge H.J. Cummings that he had seen blood on Milgaard's clothes, but added that Milgaard had said something to the effect of "I've got blood on my clothes" before he changed. He repeated his remark that Milgaard claimed to be a member of the Mafia, but he also added a new element the Crown wasn't expecting. Cadrain told the court that during the trip to Alberta, Milgaard had used the car's headlights to flag down a semi-trailer and then carried a suitcase over and handed it up to the driver.

The Crown didn't press the point because they weren't prepared for it. Tallis questioned a few of the witnesses but, like most defence counsel, didn't speak much for fear of revealing too much about the defence he would prepare for Milgaard's trial. In the end, the preliminary inquiry was more of a formality than an exercise in justice. Cummings ordered Milgaard to stand trial in Saskatoon's Court of Queen's Bench.

By January 19, 1970, the first day of the trial, almost everyone in Saskatoon, even Saskatchewan, knew the particulars of the case because of the media's reports from the preliminary inquiry, but no one seemed concerned that the potential jury pool in Saskatoon might be tainted. At the end of the day, 11 men and one woman were empanelled to hear Milgaard's case.

The Crown's case seemed relatively straightforward. It relied almost exclusively on Wilson's, John's and Cadrain's testimonies to link Milgaard to the crime. Crown prosecutor T.D.R. Caldwell also marched out some of the physical evidence, including photos of the crime scene and the stab wounds on Miller's body, to shock the jury. On day two of the trial, with opening arguments complete, Wilson took the stand.

As the jury watched, Wilson repeated his false testimony but tried to obscure his answers in such a way that his story wouldn't seem as damning. Although he had earlier claimed he had seen Milgaard with a knife during the drive to Calgary, he talked around exactly where on Milgaard's person he had seen the knife.

"But how would you see it if it was in his pocket, for example?" Chief Justice A.H. Bence asked at one point.

"Well, I don't know if it was in his pocket or not, but at the time I saw it," Wilson responded.

"Where was it, in his hand or—?" Bence tried.

"This I can't remember," Wilson replied.

There were other inconsistencies in Wilson's testimony that Tallis tried to focus on during cross-examination. Wilson told the jury originally that when he and Milgaard went separate ways to look for help for their stalled car, Wilson had walked approximately four or five blocks away before returning to the car and that, in total, the pair had been separated for approximately 15 minutes. This testimony was notably different from what Wilson had said at the preliminary inquiry, when he testified that he had walked roughly two blocks and been gone for a total of five minutes.

"Why do you choose to double it under oath on this occasion?" Tallis asked.

"Because since the preliminary, I have been thinking about it a lot," Wilson responded.

Tallis was hoping to show the jury that Milgaard couldn't have had enough time to leave the car, walk down the alley, find Miller, rape her, stab her 27 times and return to the vehicle in the time Wilson said he was gone.

Once Wilson finished, John took the stand and dropped a legal bombshell that would ultimately have more of an effect on Milgaard's conviction than she probably intended. When Caldwell started questioning the young woman about the road trip and what she had seen on the night of the murder, John replied with a simple answer far different from what she had told the police: she didn't remember.

After a visibly frustrated Caldwell asked that the jury be excused, he explained to Bence what was going on—that John had given a signed statement to the police and was now going against what she had written. Caldwell applied for permission to cross-examine John in front of the jury about the contents of her statement, declaring her a hostile witness. Tallis argued that doing so would essentially allow the Crown to enter her statement into evidence without having her testify at all. This would be highly prejudicial to his client and should only be done without the jury present in the courtroom. Bence ruled in favour of the Crown. The decision became a monumental one in Canadian jurisprudence, so much so that in the future, whenever an attorney cross-examined a witness on a previous statement, they referred to it as "Milgaarding the witness."

When the jury reassembled, Caldwell started reading John's own statement back to her. With each question, John replied between sobs that she simply didn't know.

"And you don't recall him stabbing her with the knife?" Caldwell asked.

"No, I don't," John replied.

"And you don't recall whether or not you saw him taking her around the corner of the alley?"

"No, I don't."

"And as I understand it, you don't even recall whether you ran after that?"

"No, I don't."

John didn't admit to anything, but in claiming a faulty memory, she had allowed Caldwell to read all of her evidence, however false it might be, into the record. It was a strategy that backfired because John's testimony had been the most incriminating of all, and the jury heard every single word of it.

Cadrain took the stand next and, unlike John, told his story exactly as he had told it to the police. Yet there were things about Cadrain that the jury didn't know. They didn't know that he'd been hallucinating, that he had seen a vision of the Virgin Mary and a snake that looked like Milgaard, which he understood to mean that Milgaard was guilty.

And the jury didn't know that Cadrain was in line to receive the $2,000 reward for Milgaard's arrest.

Tallis wondered aloud why, if Cadrain knew of all this damning evidence, he hadn't told the police about it when he was first questioned while in custody shortly after the fateful road trip.

"And, as a matter of fact, you had every opportunity to recollect that for the police in Regina, didn't you?" Tallis asked.

"I never thought nothing of it," Cadrain replied.

Where Caldwell did run into trouble at trial was trying to admit questionable physical evidence into the trial. A serology examination of the semen found at the scene of the crime had yielded a blood type—A. But the fact that pathologists were able to discern that much actually worked against their case. In order to be able to determine blood type from bodily fluids such as semen or urine, a person has to be a secretor. In other words, his or her body secretes antigens into other fluids, which allows a serologist to determine blood type based on those fluids. Eighty per cent of the population are secretors. Milgaard was one of the 20 per cent whose body didn't secrete antigens—a non-secretor. Even though his blood type was also type A, there was no way for pathologists to determine his blood type via the semen sample.

Caldwell countered this evidence by trying to argue that Milgaard might have had a condition or injury that caused his body to leak a small amount of blood into his semen, thereby explaining the presence of the antigens. The pathologist he relied on had tried using a test typically used to detect blood in urine, not in semen. Regardless, the test came back positive for a minute trace of blood. Caldwell was never able to explain definitively how blood could have ended up in the semen.

On day seven of the trial, Caldwell suddenly asked the judge to excuse the jury from the room. When the 11 men and one woman filed out, Caldwell announced that two new witnesses had come forward with evidence that amounted to a confession by Milgaard. After screening the testimony, Bence allowed the two men to take the stand in succession.

Both Craig Melnyk and George Lapchuk were known drug users with criminal records, but the story they had to tell was too good for the Crown to pass up. Melnyk took the stand first and told the jury that one night in May 1969, he and Lapchuk, both friends of Wilson's, along with Milgaard, had been partying in a motel room with two girls named Deborah Hall and Ute Frank. The television was on and the 11:00 news started, which contained a short news item on the Miller murder. Both Melnyk and Lapchuk told the court that after the report, Milgaard, who was seated on the bed, grabbed a pillow and started demonstrating to everyone in the room how he had stabbed Miller, apparently going so far as to state "I killed her" approximately 14 times during the display.

Neither Hall nor Frank was called to corroborate the testimony. Tallis, who had a few days' warning that the pair were coming to the trial, did his best to discredit both witnesses, eliciting from both that they were frequent drug users, were out on bail for armed robbery (Melnyk) and passing bad cheques (Lapchuk) and had once been asked by the police to act as paid drug informants. Painting that picture, however, did not detract from the weight of their testimonies.

The two teens were the Crown's last witnesses of substance. On January 29, Caldwell rested his case. Tallis, in response, called no evidence. He had only briefly entertained the idea of putting Milgaard on the stand, but quickly rejected it. Regardless of what he might say, Milgaard was only one person trying to discount the evidence of five witnesses. Tallis decided that his best strategy would be to outline in his summation just how improbable it was that Milgaard could have committed the crime.

In closing, Tallis pointed out several facts to the jury. He highlighted the shifting testimonies of Wilson, Cadrain and John and how all three had been remarkably inconsistent in their stories. He wondered aloud why, if Milgaard had killed Miller in such a rage, his friends saw only a few drops of blood on his pants when he changed his clothes. The police hadn't found any blood in Wilson's car. If Milgaard had done what the Crown was arguing, shouldn't he have been covered in it?

He took the jury through the timeline of the crime, trying to prove that Milgaard hadn't had enough time to commit the rape and murder. Miller, he pointed out, was last seen alive shortly before 7:00 AM, when she usually caught the bus to work. But the clerk on shift at the motel testified that Milgaard had come in around 7:10 AM to buy a map and ask for directions.

"It defies common sense that all these things happened in this short space of time," Tallis said.

When the jury returned the next day to hear their charge, Bence mirrored some of Tallis' arguments. In explaining how they could weigh the evidence put before them, Bence admitted some skepticism. He told the jury to be cautious with almost everything they had heard. He urged them to keep in mind such factors as the changing nature of Wilson's testimony, the lack of blood on Milgaard's person following the crime and that almost all of the witnesses in this case were teenagers who used drugs. He singled out Melnyk's and Lapchuk's testimonies as particularly dangerous.

"You may ask yourselves what would be the motive in these persons of dubious character inculpating the accused, which they endeavoured to do," said Bence. "You have to consider whether the fact that they are both now charged with crimes might have something to do with it."

On January 30, shortly after noon, Bence excused the jury to begin their deliberations, which lasted well into the night. The 11 men and one woman charged with Milgaard's fate were sequestered at a motel overnight and then resumed deliberations the next morning.

According to *When Justice Fails: The David Milgaard Story*, written by Carl Karp and Cecil Rosner, the jury started their deliberations evenly split on the issue of Milgaard's guilt. As time wore on, all but one had come to a decision. On January 31, the last dissenter finally conceded and voted with the rest.

Shortly after noon, 24 hours after they had been charged, the jury returned to the courtroom and announced their verdict. David Milgaard, they ruled, was guilty of non-capital murder.

Bence's response was swift and automatic.

"Stand up please. The sentence in this case is mandatory. You are sentenced to imprisonment for life. Remove the prisoner."

One year later, Cadrain received his $2,000 reward.

~

By 1971, Milgaard had exhausted all legal avenues to clear his name.

In January of that year, the Saskatchewan Court of Appeal dismissed his appeal. Shortly afterwards, the Supreme Court of Canada announced it would not hear Milgaard's case.

At about the same time the criminal justice system slammed the door closed on Milgaard, it also incarcerated another man whose name would become forever linked with Milgaard's. In May of 1971, Larry Fisher, a construction worker living in Saskatoon, was sentenced to 13 years in prison on two counts of rape. While working on a job in Manitoba, Fisher had attacked a 19-year-old woman near the University of Manitoba campus. One month later, he also attacked an 18-year-old on her way home from a dance club. It was during this second rape that Fisher made the mistake that would land him in jail. When he grabbed the woman, he pulled her in between two houses to finish the attack. The residents of the homes were still inside and called the police when they heard the woman scream. The police arrived in time to arrest Fisher. During his interrogation, Fisher admitted to both rapes, as well as four other rapes in Saskatoon. The judge slapped Fisher with a 13-year sentence for the two rapes in Winnipeg. A judge in Regina imposed three more four-year sentences and one six-month sentence, which were to be served concurrently.

Although the police never knew it until later, Fisher had been questioned in relation to Miller's murder. Not only did he ride the same bus as Miller to work, but he also lived in Cadrain's basement with his wife, Linda.

No one seemed to notice that Fisher's assaults closely mirrored how Miller had been killed. He typically grabbed a woman from behind, threatened her with a knife and dragged her into an isolated area such as alley. Strangely enough, the police never notified any of his five victims that Fisher had been arrested or convicted.

~

Milgaard couldn't stand prison.

Corrections Canada first housed him at the Prince Albert Penitentiary in Saskatchewan, but Milgaard fought for a transfer. His family had moved back to Winnipeg after the trial, and he wanted to be moved to the Stony Mountain Institution so that he could be closer to them. The prison authorities responded by shipping him out to Dorchester Penitentiary in New Brunswick with the promise that he might be moved to Stony.

Jailed for life for a crime he denied committing, Milgaard became despondent and suicidal. He cut his wrists on more than one occasion and swallowed small pieces of wire, and required emergency surgery as a result. He was written up repeatedly for violating institutional rules by threatening his guards or refusing to obey their commands. Yet while Milgaard, convicted as a rapist, was considered within the prison community to be second only to child molesters as the lowest of the low, he was seldom subject to the kind of "prison justice" that other such inmates often were.

Milgaard knew his chances of ever seeing the outside world again were slim. There was no mandatory minimum for his parole eligibility, meaning that corrections officials would be responsible for determining when, if ever, he would be paroled. But there was one large obstacle in Milgaard's path—he refused to admit his guilt. Acknowledging one's crime and showing some insight into its consequences is considered an important factor in determining whether or not a criminal can be paroled. So long as Milgaard maintained his innocence, he was condemned to languish behind bars.

And so on March 24, 1973, with his transfer to Stony looking increasingly less likely and his hopes of parole practically non-existent, Milgaard took matters into his own hands.

Milgaard joined up with Harvey and Michel Satel, both convicted of armed robbery, who were planning a jail break. After creating three dummies to put in their beds to fool the guards doing checks at night, they snuck away to the gym during exercise time. The plan was to wait until everyone else was gone and then sneak into the yard, where another inmate would help boost them over the prison wall.

Their plans were interrupted by a sharp-nosed guard dog that caught their scent while they were holed up inside the gym. The trio rushed the dog's handler, overpowered him and forced the guard to make regular radio calls to his superiors stating that everything was fine. In the early morning hours, the three used an extension cord to climb over the wall and run for freedom, leaving the dog handler behind.

Shortly afterwards, the local police received a call from the family members of an older couple who lived near the prison. The family was concerned about the short, perfunctory answers the couple were giving over the phone. News of the escape had already leaked to the press, and the police had roadblocks set up throughout the area. Responding to the call, the police surrounded the house and waited. Eventually, three men dashed from the home into the woods. Milgaard and the Satels were arrested shortly afterwards. They hadn't harmed the couple in any way, only eating some food and using their laundry facilities to dry their clothes. Prison officials found that the Satels, not Milgaard, were the masterminds behind the prison break, and a court sentenced him to only an additional three years for being unlawfully at large, as well as a concurrent six-year term for armed robbery.

Within two years, Milgaard's escape attempt had seemingly been forgotten. He was transferred back to Prince Albert in 1974 and was eventually shipped to Stony in 1976, where he could be closer to his family. It provided him some small relief, and Milgaard started to behave a bit better. He had upgraded his schooling in Dorchester and had taken some courses from the University of New Brunswick. Prison officials even approved him for a three-hour temporary escorted pass to visit his sick grandmother.

But Milgaard's mental health was at issue. He was transferred to the Regional Psychiatric Centre in Saskatoon for a one-month assessment, where a psychiatrist concluded that he exhibited some traits of a psychopathic personality. Officials sent him from Saskatoon to a mental health institution in Penetanguishene, Ontario, for treatment, but he was discharged from that centre when the staff concluded that there was no evidence of a disorder. Eventually, he was sent to another mental health facility in British Columbia. He still refused to say he had killed Miller and was therefore never granted parole.

On August 22, 1980, Milgaard received another temporary escorted pass to attend his brother's birthday party. The family assembled at an apartment building in Winnipeg, where Milgaard's escort, Ben Dozenko, left him alone with his sister to play pool for a few minutes. When he returned, Milgaard was gone. A large-scale manhunt ensued. The police released Milgaard's name and likeness to the public, warning that he was likely dangerous.

He wasn't, of course, but the police didn't believe that. Milgaard's freedom lasted 76 days, during which time he found work as an encyclopedia salesman in Toronto, got himself a room to live in and even met a girl he became romantically involved with. The job fizzled out, and Milgaard soon found himself panhandling. He worked and lived under the assumed name of David McAdam, but it wasn't enough to keep the police at bay. Acting on a tip that Milgaard was in Toronto, officers found him and tried to arrest him. Milgaard ran. The chase came to an end when an officer fired his service revolver as the escapee was fleeing. The bullet hit Milgaard in the buttock.

∽

North Battleford is a small community in Saskatchewan. So when Larry Fisher received statutory release on January 6, 1980, after serving two-thirds of his sentence, and decided to move to the community to live with his mother, the RCMP knew about it instantly.

The only thing different about Fisher when he arrived in North Battleford was that he was now single. His wife, Linda, had divorced him in 1976. He had been repeatedly picked on and abused by other inmates in prison because of the nature of his crimes. During his time in jail, Fisher had never received any counselling. He didn't understand the nature of his crimes and didn't know how to control his urges. It was only a matter of time before he would strike again.

On March 31, a 56-year-old woman was on her way home when a man attacked and raped her. The crime was particularly brutal. The attacker slit the woman's throat with a knife and stabbed her several times. The victim managed to get to a nearby house to get help and miraculously survived the attack. Because of the small size of the community, the RCMP had a good idea of who their main suspect was. When they arrived at Fisher's mother's house, they found him washing the blood off his boots.

Fisher eventually pleaded guilty to charges of rape and attempted murder and received a 10-year sentence. His now-estranged wife, having learned of the news, found herself staring at a flyer she had received. It offered a $10,000 reward for any information that could help prove Milgaard was innocent of the rape and murder of Miller.

Linda remembered much of the night of January 31, 1969, and the ensuing day, how close they lived to the crime scene and how Larry had refused to go to work the next day. She also remembered that one of her paring knives had gone missing around that time.

With flyer in hand, Linda walked into the offices of the Saskatoon police and gave a statement saying she believed her ex-husband could have been responsible for Miller's death. The police took one page of notes, filed it away and promptly forgot about it.

∾

Joyce Milgaard was banking on her son's innocence. Literally.

She had started circulating a flyer, offering a $10,000 reward for any information that could exonerate her son. The money would come from her RRSPs.

Milgaard's conviction had been hard on the family. Joyce had divorced David's father and now devoted most of her waking hours to poring over witness statements and transcripts of the trial. In January 1981, with the help of freelance journalist Peter Carlyle-Gordge, she began hunting down the witnesses whose testimony had landed her son behind bars.

She started with Wilson, who told her the police had found him after they talked to Cadrain. Wilson offered little in the way of assistance, but did state he was no longer certain Milgaard could have murdered Miller. John was unhelpful, meeting with Joyce in the presence of an attorney and asserting that she still didn't remember what had happened that night.

Joyce's biggest break came when she was finally able to track down Deborah Hall, one of the girls who had been present during the night of Milgaard's so-called confession at the motel room, but had never been called to testify. Hall confirmed for

Joyce that the story was, in fact, a lie. Milgaard had made a joke about the stabbing but had never re-enacted it with his pillow.

Cadrain, who had now been treated for paranoid schizophrenia, admitted to Joyce that the police had put substantial pressure on him and that he still believed that Milgaard was a member of the Mafia.

Joyce had a lot of hints that something had gone wrong, a lot of loose ends that raised more questions. But to date, none of the key witnesses had offered any evidence that she could point to as incontrovertible proof that her son was innocent. She eventually turned to a local lawyer named Hersh Wolch for help, who passed the file on to a young lawyer named David Asper. Right away, Asper started working almost exclusively on Joyce's behalf.

Asper knew that David's only chance of vindication came from the highest levels of government. Under the Criminal Code of Canada, the minister of justice had the authority in instances where a miscarriage of justice was perceived to have occurred to order a new trial. With the Supreme Court of Canada having refused to hear Milgaard's appeal in 1971, Asper knew his new client's only hope would come through contacting the minister.

Asper's first action, after reviewing trial notes and transcripts, was to ask Hall to sign a sworn affidavit. In the document, Hall asserted that there had been five people in the motel room when the news came on and a piece about Miller played. When Melnyk had said to Milgaard, "You did it, didn't you,"

Milgaard responded, "Oh, yeah, right," He just happened to have been fluffing a pillow at the same time.

Asper also commissioned forensic pathologist Dr. James Ferris to analyze the physical evidence that had been presented at trial. Milgaard had hoped the pathologist might also be able to use a new identification technique called DNA matching to exonerate him. The technology, however, was young, and the sample too small to measure. Ferris did conclude in his report, however, that much of the testimony about physical evidence at the trial had been shoddy, if not suspect. Ferris stated he knew of no cases in which a suspect had secreted blood into his own semen; it stood to reason, he said, that the sample had been contaminated by blood at the scene of the crime. He also stated there was a high likelihood that the entire crime scene had been contaminated by the police in the first few hours of their investigation.

He pointed to the stab wounds in Miller's lung, which had been ruled as the official cause of death. It was quite likely, Ferris wrote, that Miller could still have been conscious for up to 15 minutes after injury. Consequently, "the circumstances of the rape/murder were complex, probably prolonged, and in my opinion, incapable of having occurred within the time frame suggested."

In December 1988, Asper gathered together Hall's affidavit, Ferris' report and a succinct, sharply aimed attack of the Crown's case, packaged them together and fired them off to Ottawa for the minister of justice to review.

Milgaard's crime was so notorious that any attempt to have it re-investigated was bound to provoke media attention. Joyce and Asper welcomed it, using print, radio and television to help make their case. As a result, the investigation into Miller's death and the circumstances surrounding Milgaard's conviction began to take on a life of their own.

In 1989, a member of the jury stepped forward and claimed that he had been the last person to switch sides in the jury room. He told the media he should not have been selected as a juror because at the time he was mentally unfit to serve.

The biggest break, however, came in 1990, when an anonymous tipster suggested that Asper and Joyce might want to look into the background of a convicted sex offender named Larry Fisher.

The investigation was taxing Joyce's resources, but she got some help. A friend who worked for an American group named Centurion, which specialized in investigating wrongful convictions, secured the services of a private investigator named Paul Henderson and also offered to pay his fee. Henderson's first stop was Cando, Saskatchewan, where Linda Fisher now lived. It was there that word of Linda's statement to the police nine years before first came to light. Even though she knew the $10,000 reward was no longer being offered, Linda signed an affidavit confirming everything she had already told the police. Asper diligently forwarded the new information on to the minister of justice.

Henderson started logging some serious travel time from that point on. He managed to track down Wilson, Cadrain and John once again. Though Cadrain himself did not meet with Henderson, his brother told the investigator that whatever Cadrain had undergone during his questioning had upset his mental balance. He talked about his brother's diagnosis of schizophrenia and of the ulcers he battled, along with the vision of the Virgin Mary and the snake.

Henderson noted the information as a snapshot of Cadrain's state of mind and kept on travelling. He next dropped in on Wilson in Nakusp, BC, just south of Revelstoke. Over the course of an eight-hour interview, Wilson shocked Henderson by recanting every single portion of his trial testimony. Wilson told Henderson he had not seen blood on Milgaard's pants, had not seen him with a knife that night and had not seen John in hysterics. He had not seen Milgaard throw a cosmetics case from the car and had never heard him say that he had "hit a girl." Wilson went on to say that he and Milgaard had never been separated for any longer than a couple of minutes.

Buoyed by Wilson's testimony, Henderson hit the road again, tracking John down. Her parents, however, refused to let the investigator talk to her, going so far as to file a harassment complaint with the RCMP. Undaunted, Henderson again went to see Cadrain, who gave him a sworn statement that, while he had seen blood on Milgaard's pants, the police had put him "through hell and mental torture" during the ensuing questioning.

Asper commissioned a second pathologist, this one Chief Medical Examiner of Manitoba Peter Markesteyn, to review the evidence again. His analysis confirmed what Ferris had already stated. Furthermore, Markesteyn went on to state that the lumps found at the Miller crime scene could have been dog urine, not semen. He stated that male dog urine sometimes contains semen.

As the case began to break open, the media continued to hop on board, trying to flesh out the story. Fisher himself gave a terse, fragmented interview to CBC in which he denied killing Miller. Saskatchewan police chief Joe Penkala issued a public statement condemning the new investigation and its effect on the victims. Detectives who had investigated Milgaard denied ever subjecting the witnesses to any mistreatment.

Yet for all the coverage, Milgaard's application to Minister of Justice Kim Campbell just seemed to be sitting there. When Campbell visited Winnipeg on May 14, 1990, Joyce approached her and tried to talk to her. In front of the media, Campbell brushed past Joyce, telling her, "If you want your son to have a fair hearing, don't approach me personally." The image was cemented in the minds of the media—the brusque, uncaring bureaucrat turning her nose up at a caring, heartbroken mother. The intensity of the case continued to build.

It took until February 27, 1991, for Campbell to render her decision, and when she did, the outcry was palpable. The minister announced that she had denied the application. Her staff tore into Milgaard's application, repudiating every argument made with facts submitted mostly at trial. They questioned Wilson's motives for switching his story, argued that the forensic evidence presented at trial had not been much of a factor in Milgaard's conviction and stated that Hall's affidavit regarding the motel room confession still indicated a confession of sorts on Milgaard's part. Larry Fisher's record, the department wrote, wasn't proof that he could have killed Miller, and while Asper had argued that the time frame for the killing was incorrect, he hadn't provided any new evidence proving the fact.

Milgaard was devastated and sank into a deep depression. Rather than give up, Joyce and Asper started marshalling their forces again for a new application. They tracked down all of Fisher's victims, many of whom didn't know he had ever been arrested and jailed, and assembled a map of the locations of their attacks, most of which were close to the area where Miller's body was found. A woman in Toronto contacted them to say she had been attacked by a man the same morning Miller had died. He had come running up, grabbed her between the legs and then run away when she screamed. She had reported the matter to the Saskatoon police but had never heard of any follow-up.

Joyce had also recruited some surprising supporters. Miller's family had joined the campaign to free Milgaard.

With what little new information they had, Asper and Joyce forwarded a second application to Campbell, asking her to order a new trial for Milgaard. On September 5, 1991, the only person in Canada more powerful than Campbell in regard to justice came to Winnipeg for a visit. Joyce waited outside a hotel, hoping to impress upon Prime Minister Brian Mulroney the importance of her cause. Rather than shy away from Joyce as Campbell had the previous year, Mulroney went right up to her and praised her bravery and courage. While he said he couldn't speak for Campbell, Mulroney stated, "I'll be talking to her when I get back."

Campbell later admitted that she was blindsided by Mulroney's intervention, but had little recourse. The prime minister placed a personal call to the Stony Mountain Institution, and shortly afterwards, Corrections Canada transferred Milgaard to Rockford Institution, a minimum-security prison.

On November 29, Campbell convened a press conference in Toronto and stated that based on other evidence submitted with the new application, she was ordering the Supreme Court of Canada to review Milgaard's case to determine whether or not a new trial was warranted.

The wait wasn't yet over. Milgaard was still convicted of murder. He couldn't be granted bail until the Supreme Court had dealt with the questions Campbell had submitted. There were only two: (1) "Does the continued conviction of David Milgaard in Saskatoon, Saskatchewan, for the murder of Gail Miller, in the opinion of the court, constitute a miscarriage of justice?" and (2) "What remedial action under the Criminal Code, if any, is advisable?"

History was not on Milgaard's side. The Supreme Court of Canada debates weighty issues of law. It is not intended as a criminal court and was not set up to hear from witnesses. The justices typically convene only to hear arguments on points of law from lawyers. Only twice in its history had the court ever reviewed a murder conviction—once for Thomas Coffin and once for Stephen Truscott. The court had upheld both men's convictions. Coffin had been executed.

On January 21, 1992, Chief Justice Antonio Lamer and justices Peter Cory, Beverly McLachlin, Frank Iacobucci and John Sopinka convened the review of Milgaard's 1970 murder conviction. Subpoenaed to testify, Milgaard was transferred to a halfway house in Ottawa, which offered even more freedom than he was used to. Unfortunately, that freedom and Milgaard's carefree attitude would cause him trouble during the review.

Milgaard was the first witness. His answer to the first question was telling.

"Did you kill Gail Miller?

"I did not kill Gail Miller."

For a man who had spent 23 years waiting to tell his side of the story, Milgaard's testimony was brief, lasting only 45 minutes. It was the remaining witnesses who would try to corroborate his story. Wilson again recanted his original testimony and revealed for the first time that he too had applied for the $2,000 reward offered for Milgaard's conviction. John performed just as she had at the original trial, claiming she couldn't remember any of the pertinent details. Larry Fisher took the stand, but kept his answers short, refusing to implicate himself.

Milgaard, however, would not get to watch the remainder of the hearing. One night, he stepped outside the halfway house in Ottawa during a downpour and didn't report back by curfew. The halfway house staff promptly notified the police, who issued a Canada-wide warrant for his arrest. The search ended five hours later when the staff at the halfway house staff found Milgaard on the back porch of the facility, enjoying the feeling of rain on his skin. He was promptly transferred back to Stony Mountain and wasn't permitted to attend the rest of hearing.

It took the Supreme Court four months to come to a decision once the hearing closed. On April 14, the justices released their ruling, which proved to be a mixed bag of results for Milgaard. While the court maintained that, from its perspective, Milgaard had received a fair trial in 1970 and that it didn't believe he was necessarily innocent, it did rule that the evidence supporting Milgaard's innocence that came to light after the trial might have affected the jury's verdict had that evidence been revealed during the trial. The court recommended that the government order a new trial. It also took the unusual step of recommending that, in the event that a new trial found Milgaard guilty again, the minister should pardon Milgaard for the crime, which would exonerate him and remove Miller's murder from his criminal record. The court wrote that "some sympathetic consideration of David Milgaard's current situation is in order."

Campbell quickly quashed the original verdict and ordered a new trial. The government of Saskatchewan announced that it would enter a stay in the charge against Milgaard, effectively renouncing any commitment to trying him again. On April 16, Milgaard walked away from jail a free man, but not necessarily an innocent one in the eyes of the courts.

"It feels good to be out forever," he said.

Saskatchewan's provincial government made no bones about the fact that it thought Milgaard was probably guilty. Along with staying the charge, it had stated that it would not order any kind of commission of inquiry and would not compensate Milgaard for the time he spent behind bars.

It was a difficult time for Milgaard. Unequipped to deal with a life of no restraints after 23 years in jail, he took to his old ways, hitchhiking across the country. In October 1993, he was charged in Vancouver for being drunk and disorderly. The next fall, he was arrested for stealing a public utilities commission van and driving it into a swamp. He was arrested a third time in Toronto for breaking some windows, but the charges were withdrawn after he paid a $200 fine. Milgaard's mental state was tenuous—he had been diagnosed with bipolar disorder and sometimes didn't take his medications.

Asper had resigned shortly after the Supreme Court decision, passing Milgaard's file on to Greg Rodin, who was working on Milgaard's behalf to get him compensation for the 23 years lost to jail and to restore his good name. In March 1993, Rodin filed suit against two Crown prosecutors, three police officers and the City of Saskatoon for Milgaard's conviction.

Money, however, wasn't Milgaard's chief concern. He wanted his name cleared. By 1995, the technology used to match DNA had evolved sufficiently that pathologists believe it could be used to finally determine who had murdered Miller. In May 1997, after two years of negotiations with the government, samples of Milgaard's blood, along with samples from a man Miller had been out with the night before her death, Wilson, and Larry Fisher were sent to the Forensic Science Services Lab near London, England. Remarkably, pathologists found a large semen stain on the dress Miller had been wearing the night she died. Extracting the DNA from the semen, they then compared it with the four samples.

The match was quick and definitive. The odds were one in 400 million that the semen belonged to one of the four men. It was Larry Fisher, not David Milgaard.

"There is no justice in being locked up behind bars for something you have not done," Milgaard later said in a statement. "How would you feel if no one would tell the truth about you?"

Immediately afterwards, the Saskatchewan government stepped forward with an interim compensation payment of $250,000 and the promise of a public inquiry. On January 17, 2005, the inquiry opened hearings under the authority of Alberta Court of Queen's Bench Justice Edward P. McCallum. Between that date and October 4, 2006, McCallum listened to the testimony of approximately 130 witnesses, trying to determine how Milgaard had been convicted of a crime he hadn't committed. As of the writing of this book, McCallum has yet to tender his final report.

Milgaard negotiated a $10-million compensation agreement with the federal government and the province of Saskatchewan, with the province chipping in $6 million and Ottawa $4 million. He remained a fixture in the news during his hearings, when he practically refused to testify before the inquiry exploring his own wrongful conviction, claiming the thought of having to do so made him ill. Eventually McCallum agreed to allow Milgaard to testify by videotape.

Fisher tried to run after pathologists matched his DNA to the semen stain found on Miller's dress, but he didn't get far. He was arrested in Calgary in 1997, and his case went swiftly to trial. On November 22, 1999, after 13 hours of deliberations, a jury found him guilty of killing and raping Miller. He was sentenced to life in prison.

Chapter Two

Donald Marshall Junior

Near Sydney, Nova Scotia
May 28, 1971

There were no cars stopping for Maynard Chant that night. The 14-year-old native of Louisbourg, Nova Scotia, was just looking for a ride home. He walked the side of the road, haphazardly dangling a thumb into traffic, watching as each car zipped by without slowing. All he wanted to do was go home and go to bed, maybe try to sleep off or drink away the events of the evening.

But home was still a long way off.

He looked down at his clothes, which were spattered with blood, and picked at them with his free hand, which was also stained crimson, but the blood was stubborn and refused to come off. He sniffed and turned his attention back to the road, trying not to remember how the night had gone so horribly wrong.

He hadn't been expecting much that night because his parents had dragged him to church again. Like most teenagers,

Chant had no interest in spiritual matters, and growing up in a Pentecostal family was religion, super-sized. So rather than spend his entire night locked up in a Sydney church, muttering words he didn't really believe, Chant had decided to slip away from his family and hit the road. He had a friend visiting from out of town and felt there were better things he could be doing with his time than asking for God's blessings.

But Chant was too late. The last bus from Sydney to Louisbourg had already left. Faced with the options of returning to church or hitchhiking home, Chant had chosen to hitch. He had just cut through Wentworth Park heading to George Street when Donald came out of nowhere.

Another car whipped by, and Chant blinked as gravel and debris washed over him. He closed his eyes and again saw Donald thrusting a bleeding arm into his face and babbling excitedly about some stabbing back in the park. He said something about an old guy dressed like a priest and a knife, and that Sandy had been stabbed and was still back there.

At the sound of tires on gravel, Chant opened his eyes. He turned to see a police car pulling up beside him. The blood on his clothes and his hands flared in the car's headlights, and the officer behind the wheel wasted no time in asking him if he knew anything about what had happened at Wentworth Park.

"Yeah, I seen it all," said Chant.

It was a lie. He hadn't seen it all, and he didn't know what had happened. But Chant didn't see what harm telling one lie could possibly do.

More than 10 years later, Chant found God. And he knew that this lie had been just one more nail in the coffin of an innocent man.

~

No one could say that Donald Marshall Junior was an upstanding citizen as young man.

The Mi'kmaq Native, who lived on the Membertou Reserve, just outside of Sydney, was getting into trouble almost as soon as he hit adolescence. He'd been expelled from school at the age of 15 for hitting a teacher. He and his friends from the reserve often spent their time drinking, fighting and committing random acts of senseless vandalism. On one occasion, they had caused $19,000 worth of damage at St. Anthony Daniel Cemetery by knocking over headstones and lighting off blasting caps. He'd already done a four-month stint in jail for supplying liquor to a minor and been fined for drinking in public.

Without much in the way of a future, Marshall now worked as an apprentice for his father, whose reputation in Nova Scotia often preceded him. Donald Marshall Senior worked as a plasterer, but he was also the Grand Chief of the 5,000-strong Mi'kmaq nation in Nova Scotia, the spiritual leader of the First

Nations group. It was a position that young Marshall could one day inherit.

But Marshall was happier spending his days in Wentworth Park in Sydney, drinking and smoking cigarettes. He felt no shame in panhandling or rolling total strangers if he needed money. He preferred to let his size and strength carry him through life.

The night of May 28, 1971, was looking good for Marshall. There was a big dance at St. Joseph's Parish, and he and his friends were going to head over after having a few drinks first. They started with some rum at a friend's house, but Marshall became separated from his friends when they left for the dance. Working his way over on his own steam, Marshall decided to stop first in Wentworth Park to see if any of his friends were around.

Sandy Seale had already been to the dance and was turned away. The place was packed, and they were refusing people at the door. The accomplished hockey player and bright student was working his way through the park to get back home when he ran into Marshall.

The two boys knew each other. They had seen one another at other dances, and Marshall's father had once worked on Seale's father's house. When Seale told Marshall that the dance was sold out, Marshall asked Seale if he wanted to do a little panhandling to make some money. Seale agreed. It was a fatal decision.

The pair spied two men stumbling their way across the park. It looked like it would be an easy roll. One of the men was short and visibly older, with wild grey hair. He was dressed in some sort of robe and walked with a cane. His younger partner didn't look like he could handle himself.

Marshall and Seale approached the pair smoothly, Marshall chatting them up and hinting he and Seale needed some money. Neither of the men seemed to hear him, but the older one with the cane invited the pair back to his house for a drink. At that moment, two of Marshall's friends appeared on the scene, calling to him. Patricia Harriss was supporting her visibly drunk boyfriend, Terry Gushue, who needed a light for his cigarette. Marshall obliged them, Harriss and Gushue moved on, and Marshall turned back to the strange-looking pair.

Marshall again repeated his request for money. When the pair didn't react, Marshall grabbed the younger man by the arm. Seale turned to the old man with the cane and ordered him to empty his pockets.

"Dig, man. Dig," Seale prompted him.

There was an explosion of action. The old man's hand disappeared briefly and then lunged forward and connected with Seale's stomach. The young black man gasped and stumbled backwards, his hands flying to his abdomen. Marshall stood momentarily perplexed, released his captive and wheeled backwards as the old man's hand slashed at him. He heard fabric tearing, felt a burn erupt on his left arm. Marshall slipped once on the grass and then stood and bolted, running for his life.

Behind him, Seale had slumped to the ground, still clutching his stomach. As Marshall disappeared into the night, so too did the old man and his young companion.

~

Retired RCMP officer Marvel Mattson was trying to get to sleep when he heard a commotion on his front lawn shortly after midnight. He peeked out the window and saw two young men standing outside. One was clutching his arm and talking excitedly. The words "stabbing" and "Wentworth Park" immediately piqued the old peace officer's interest. After listening a short while longer, Mattson reached for the phone and placed a call to the Sydney city police.

~

Chant didn't know what to think as he and Marshall careened back through Wentworth Park. After Marshall ran into Chant and told him what had happened, they had decided to pile into the nearest car and head back to the park to check on Seale.

What they found was horrifying. Seale was huddled on the ground with a small group of people clustered around him. A dark pool spread out from his torso, soaking the grass. When Chant went to cover Seale's wound with his shirt, he saw and felt intestines moving under his hands.

"I'm going to die," Seale whispered. Chant didn't know what to say.

Marshall and some onlookers took off into the night, running up to a nearby house and asking the residents to call an ambulance. The homeowner called the police first, who already knew there was something going on. Within minutes, a police car pulled up beside the park to find Marshall standing in the middle of the street. No sooner had the officers exited the car than the young Native began telling them what had happened. As the officers hustled into the park to check on Seale, Marshall blurted out a rudimentary description of his attackers, "a tall fellow and a short fellow with white hair."

Moments later a second car pulled up, but still no ambulance. The "bus," it turned out, had been delayed by a severe traffic accident. When it did arrive, strong hands pulled Chant away from Seale, and the paramedics quickly scooped Seale off the ground and onto a stretcher. They loaded him into the back of the ambulance and roared off for the hospital. None of the officers at the scene thought to ride in the back with Seale.

Three police cars sat nearby as members of the Sydney Police Department tried to figure out what had happened. A pair of officers directed Marshall into the back of their squad car and took off for the hospital so the young man could have his arm examined. Despite a few whispered words, none of the officers who had responded to the incident bothered circulating Marshall's description of the attacker. No one searched the crime scene. As the people who had crowded around Seale started trickling out of the park once the ambulance took off, no one bothered to stop them to ask for statements.

No one bothered talking to Maynard Chant, either. He took his shirt and started walking home in a daze, hoping someone would stop and give him a ride. A truck picked him up, but the driver wasn't going very far and dropped him only a few blocks away. An exhausted and scared Chant stuck his thumb out again and started hitching for another ride. The next car to pull up belonged to the police.

A few blocks away, Roy Ebsary stormed into the house he shared with his common-law wife, Mary, and their two children, Greg and Donna. Behind him, a wild-eyed young man named Jimmy MacNeil followed in his wake. The pair reeked of alcohol. Mary kept her attention fixed on the television, sensing that her husband was in one of his foul moods. Young Donna, however, paused on the staircase as she made her way to bed and watched her father shuffle into the kitchen.

"You saved my life, man," MacNeil said.

"Don't say anything," Ebsary replied, stowing his cane and walking to the sink. As Donna watched, her 14-year-old mind grasping to understand what she was seeing, her father pulled a knife from beneath the shawl he wore and started washing it under the running water. From where Donna stood, she could see the water in the sink turn red instantly.

~

Seale was in bad shape when he arrived at Sydney City Hospital.

Dr. Mohammed Ali Naqvi understood immediately how grave the situation was as soon as the paramedics wheeled the young man's stretcher in the door of the hospital. Seale had no pulse, no blood pressure and was on the verge of full-blown shock. Naqvi immediately started feeding Seale pints of blood intravenously while prepping the young man for emergency surgery. A squad of police officers appeared at the hospital, asking if they could try to interview Seale before he went under the knife. Naqvi refused, knowing Seale's time was running out.

The hospital staff quickly wheeled the teen into surgery and opened him up. What they found was grim. The path of the wound sliced through the entire gastrointestinal area, ending just short of the backbone, and the entire abdominal cavity was awash in blood. After quickly repairing what damage he could, Naqvi stitched Seale's stomach closed.

But the bleeding didn't stop, forcing Naqvi to go back in. During the second surgery, the surgeon found a half-inch puncture in Seale's aorta, the major blood vessel that carries blood from the heart to the rest of the body. Naqvi stitched the puncture closed and then turned his attention to Seale's bowels.

Deprived of blood, the entire area was turning gangrenous. Again the surgeon closed up his patient. Seale was placed on an artificial respirator. Over the next 20 hours, his body sucked up 27 pints of blood.

Marshall was also being treated in the hospital. The four-inch gash in his arm had stopped bleeding but still required stitches. Shortly after his wound was attended to, two police officers asked him to accompany them to the lobby. They had picked up two suspects and wanted Marshall to identify them. Marshall's hopes were immediately dashed. Both the men in police custody were too young.

As he left the hospital, Marshall walked past Chant, who was telling an officer his version of the events. Detective Michael MacDonald wasn't impressed. Despite the youth's earlier assertion that he'd "seen it all," the officer concluded that Chant knew nothing of what had happened in the park. Chant was escorted back to the Sydney police station to wait for his father while Marshall was driven back to Membertou.

At 8:00 PM the next day, Seale died without identifying his killer.

⌇

Murder was not a common occurrence in Sydney, Nova Scotia.

The last such incident had taken place more than five years earlier, when a 70-year-old man had been found dead in the basement of his restaurant. He had been beaten about the head. The cash register was missing. The case had never been solved.

Sergeant of Detectives John MacIntyre had worked on that case and was now the investigating officer in charge of Seale's murder. He had little to work with when he arrived at work the following morning. There were absolutely no leads. They had a brief description of the attackers from Marshall and a bloody tissue that had been recovered in Wentworth Park. In a desperate search for the murder weapon, MacIntyre ordered the creeks in Wentworth Park drained, but nothing turned up. Officers tracked down several teens who had been at the dance the night before, but none had seen what happened. Frustrated, MacIntyre asked Marshall to come down to the station.

Marshall and MacIntyre had a bit of a history. The detective had interviewed Marshall when he and his friends had vandalized the graveyard, but Marshall hadn't been charged. It's alleged that MacIntyre also worked on a case in which a young woman accused Marshall of rape. The file, however, was destroyed in a fire, and MacIntyre later denied any involvement.

For a man with few leads, MacIntyre started developing his own ideas early on about what had happened in the park. It was now almost one full day since the stabbing had occurred, and no one had taken an official statement from Marshall as of yet. Rather than do so, MacIntyre asked Marshall to view a police lineup, but the young man just shook his head at the seven people in front of him, saying none of the men were his attackers. MacIntyre asked him to hang around the police station, which Marshall did until later that evening. With no other leads, MacIntyre, accompanied by Detective MacDonald, drove out to Louisbourg to have another talk with Chant.

The driver of the truck who had given Chant a quick ride after the stabbing had called the police and told them he thought Chant knew something about the murder. Even though MacDonald had already informally interviewed Chant, MacIntyre decided to have another crack at him. With Chant's mother's permission, the pair of detectives marched the teen into the back of their police car and started asking him questions about what had happened.

But what Chant told the officers stood in stark contrast to what he had already recounted. When first interviewed, he'd said that he had been walking down the street when Marshall came running up to him and told him what had happened. When Chant recited his version of events this time, he made one substantial change: he insisted to both officers that he had been present during the stabbing, even though he hadn't been. MacIntyre promptly drove Chant back to Sydney, where Chant filled out a formal written statement about the night's events.

According to his new story, Chant had been crossing the railroad tracks near Byng Avenue when he saw Seale and Marshall talking with two men. He described the men as tall, wearing dark clothing. The foursome, said Chant, had been talking near Crescent Street when one of the unknown men pulled out a knife and stabbed Seale.

Chant's statement was enough for MacIntyre to call Marshall back to the station on May 30 to finally take a formal statement. But in his detailed account of the stabbing, Marshall omitted one important fact. He never told the police exactly why he and Seale had approached the pair of men in the park in the first place.

According to Marshall, he and Seale had been standing near the band shelter in the park when two men came over and asked them for cigarettes. Marshall said he asked the two if they were priests and both men said yes. One of them had gone on to rant about how much he hated black people and Indians. Suddenly, one of the men had turned and stabbed Seale, completely unprovoked. He also slashed at Marshall before the teen had turned and run. Marshall described one of the men as tall with black hair, sporting a blue sweater, and the other one as small with grey hair, about 50 years old, wearing a blue coat.

MacIntyre wasn't buying Marshall's story. Admittedly, the sequence of events Marshall had described seemed perplexing, even unlikely. But for reasons known only to MacIntyre, he started operating on the premise that Marshall might have been the person who had stabbed Seale. He noted his suspicion in a telex dispatched to the RCMP headquarters in Halifax, in which he stated, "Marshall possibly the person responsible."

Later that night, MacIntyre stepped into an interview room to chat with another young man he was told might know something about the murder. John Pratico was a 16-year-old friend of Marshall's who had been under psychiatric care for a little more than a year. MacIntyre, however, didn't know this fact when he heard from a source that Pratico might have been drinking in the park on the night of the murder and might know something about it.

Pratico did know something about what had happened. Just the day before, he had been hanging out with Marshall at a friend's house, listening to Marshall recount the night's events. Pratico wasn't a witness, just a friend who had listened to another friend. This didn't jibe with what MacIntyre wanted to hear. The police showed up at Pratico's door the next day. Still drunk from the night before, Pratico was escorted to the police station.

It turned out that the teen had been at the dance and had been drinking quite heavily. But when he tried to tell MacIntyre that he hadn't seen any of what had happened in the park, the officer threatened him, saying Pratico could end up in jail if he didn't help the police. Unnerved and mentally off balance, Pratico quickly changed his story. By the time he left the police station, he had affixed his name to a statement in which he said he had been over by the courthouse when he heard a scream. He had looked up and seen two men jump into a white Volkswagen and drive off.

Pratico said he had seen both men at the dance earlier. One had been wearing a grey suit, the other a brown jacket. His description did not match the one Marshall had given, but that seemed to be beside the point. Pratico was released shortly afterwards.

There were more witnesses, but the investigating officers were suddenly picking and choosing which descriptions they liked. Two men responding to a media plea for witnesses came forward and said they had seen two men hanging around in the park shortly before midnight. They even described one of the men as 60 years old, with grey hair, which closely resembled what Marshall had said. But the pair were never asked to testify at trial.

The most significant testimony came from a man who had already given a statement. On June 4, two days after Seale's body was laid to rest, MacIntyre brought Pratico back to the station for further questioning and accused him of lying. MacIntyre, it seemed, had visited Wentworth Park the night before and determined that there was no way Pratico could have seen what he claimed he saw if he had been standing by the courthouse. Terrified of being imprisoned, Pratico decided to elaborate on his story instead of admitting he had never been there in the first place.

As MacIntyre jotted Pratico's statement down, the young man told him how he had been coming through the park, on the far side of the park's footbridge, when he saw Marshall and Seale standing together. Pratico had stopped behind a bush to drink a pint of beer. He said he couldn't hear them talking, but he told MacIntyre that he saw "Donald Marshall's hand going towards the left-hand side of Seale's stomach. He drove his hand in, turned it and pulled it back." After watching Seale fall to the ground, Pratico had run all the way home.

In reality, Pratico had known nothing of the stabbing until he had heard about it on the radio the morning after. He'd had to ask his mother who had been stabbed.

But MacIntyre had his own theory on what had happened at the park, and now he had eyewitness testimony supporting it. Only one person stood in the way of making it a slam-dunk—Maynard Chant.

Accompanied by Detective William Urquhart, MacIntyre again made the trip to Louisbourg and again brought Chant in for questioning. What happened during the subsequent interview has never been substantially proven. Apparently, Chant's mother, Beudah, and his probation officer, Lawrence Burke, accompanied Chant to the interview, and both their signatures later appeared on the statement Chant gave. Both denied ever signing it. Burke maintained that he hadn't even been at the Louisbourg police station. Beudah said she had been asked to leave the room during the interview, a violation of police protocol when dealing with minors. MacIntyre later admitted, under oath, that he had signed their names to the document.

Whatever the case, the story Chant gave to MacIntyre in his third interview with the police differed markedly again from his previous statements. According to Chant, both detectives told him they had information that he was lying. They said they had a witness who put him at the scene during the stabbing. And they threatened him with jail time if he didn't co-operate.

Convinced he had no other option, Chant fell into the same trap Pratico had earlier. He told MacIntyre and Urquhart exactly what they wanted to hear. In his again-revised statement, Chant said he had been walking along the tracks when he saw a dark-haired man hiding in the bushes. From there, he had seen two men standing close together on Crescent Street, one of whom he recognized as Marshall. Chant said he had heard some swearing and then saw "Marshall haul a knife from his pocket and jab the other fellow in the side of the stomach."

That Chant told the police he had seen Marshall stab Seale on the right side of the stomach while Pratico had said the left didn't matter to MacIntyre. Chant said he had run down to Byng Avenue, and Marshall had come running up to show him the cut on his arm. From that point on, Chant stuck to his original testimony of what had transpired.

But the damage was already done. MacIntyre now had two eyewitnesses claiming they saw Marshall stab Seale. After getting Chant to sign off on the revised statement, MacIntyre and Urquhart dashed back to Sydney, where they explained their case to Crown prosecutor Donald C. MacNeil. The lawyer gave the pair the go-ahead to arrest Marshall for second-degree murder.

Since the murder, the Marshalls had been staying at Whycocomagh, a reserve about 110 kilometres away, because of a series of threatening phone calls they had received at their home in Membertou. Marshall had stayed behind, but on the night of June 4, his father drove him out to Whycocomagh to be with the rest of the family. Shortly after Marshall's arrival, MacIntyre showed up and informed the young man that he was under arrest for the murder of Sandy Seale.

Donald Marshall Senior never doubted his son's innocence. He would prove to be one of the few.

~

From that moment on, Donald Marshall Junior was no longer a free man. Remanded to custody while awaiting trial, he spent his days either inside a courthouse or the county jail.

With Marshall in custody, the police were left to try to piece together the rest of their case. They got their hands on the borrowed jacket Marshall had been wearing the night of Seale's murder. They sent his bloodstained clothing for serology analysis, hoping to find Seale's blood type. Unfortunately, the samples were too small to properly analyze. MacIntyre had hoped to get more of Marshall's blood when the doctor took out his stitches, but Marshall removed the sutures himself and flushed them down the toilet. The jacket was passed on to a fibres expert for examination.

In the meantime, the police kept looking for witnesses who would corroborate what Chant and Pratico had finally told them. They were able to track down Patricia Harriss, but her statement did not support the theory of the crime so far. Harriss had been walking through Wentworth Park with her drunken boyfriend, Gushue, when Gushue asked Marshall for a light. The pair had then moved on.

When the police first interviewed Harriss, she told MacIntyre that she had seen a strange-looking man with grey hair in the park. Once MacIntyre had Chant's and Pratico's statements, however, he called Harriss in again for repeated interviews. In the second statement signed by Harriss, the only statement of hers that Marshall's defence team ever received from the police prior to trial, Harriss now said that she had seen one other person in the park, and that person was Seale. The effect was devastating for Marshall. Three eyewitnesses now put him alone in Wentworth Park with Seale. And there was no sign of the grey-haired man.

On July 5, scarcely one month after the stabbing occurred, all parties convened in Sydney for a preliminary inquiry. Over the next 23 days, 20 people testified. Of those witnesses, Marshall's defence counsel chose to cross-examine only four.

The preliminary inquiry, however, helped set the stage for some of the drama that would occur during the trial four months later. Of particular interest were the testimonies of Chant and Harriss. When asked by Crown prosecutor MacNeil if she had seen anyone else in the park with Marshall, Harriss tried to be vague, replying that she hadn't really been paying attention. In the end, she told the court she had seen one other person, but she didn't know who it had been.

When Chant took the stand, he performed exactly as the Crown wanted him to. He started by pointing out Pratico in the court as being the man he saw crouched behind the bushes in Wentworth Park. Strangely, neither the Crown nor the defence asked the presiding judge for an order excluding the witnesses from the courtroom.

Chant fell back on his concocted story of what had happened that night, explaining that he had seen two people in the park, that the two had argued and that one man had taken a knife out of his pocket and stabbed the other one in the stomach. He identified the man with the knife as Marshall.

Most of the preliminary inquiry took place under a publication ban. The defence has the right to ask for a publication ban during the inquiry, so the facts of the case aren't disclosed to the public, which could taint the prospective jury pool. Journalists who attend are allowed to report only the inquiry's outcome, how many witnesses testified and how many days the proceedings took.

The outcome of the inquiry came as no shock to anyone. The presiding judge ordered Marshall to stand trial on one count of second-degree murder, and he was ordered to remain in custody until his trial.

Six weeks later, Pratico, who had been taking Valium for some time, suffered a nervous breakdown and was hospitalized in a mental institution.

∼

On November 2, 1971, Justice J. Louis Dubinsky of the Nova Scotia Supreme Court opened the second-degree murder trial of Donald Marshall Junior. Jury selection was relatively brief. By 3:30 PM on the first day, a jury of 12 white men had been empanelled. That the defendant was of First Nations descent and the victim black seemed irrelevant.

Marshall's defence team, led by Department of Indian Affairs–appointed lawyer Moe Rosenblum and aided by Simon Khattar, had a difficult task ahead of them. Prior to the introduction of DNA testing in the late 1980s, eyewitness testimony was considered to be the most important part of any case. And in this case the Crown had two eyewitnesses to the actual crime and one witness who put the accused and victim together at the right time in the right place. It was going to be Rosenblum and Khattar's job to somehow shred the testimonies of Chant, Pratico and Harriss.

That task proved more difficult than expected, despite some inadvertent help from all three witnesses over the course of the trial. Neither of Marshall's lawyers took the time to interview any of the witnesses themselves. Had they done so, they might have been able to tease out the fact that all three had signed false statements to the police. They might also have learned that some key pieces of evidence, such as Harriss' first statement to the police, had not been included when they received their disclosure from the Crown. They were going into the trial blind, and it was their client who stood to lose the most because of it.

There was little to contend with early on. A serology expert explained to the court the difficulty in typing the blood stains on Marshall's jacket, and fibre expert Adolphus Evers explained the characteristics of two cuts he had found on the jacket.

The issue of blood did come up early in the trial, but not in relation to Marshall's jacket. MacNeil called to the stand Dr. Mohan S. Virick, who described to the jury how he had stitched up Marshall's arm in the early morning hours of May 29. According to Virick, the wound was not bleeding when he finally attended to it, but he decided to stitch it closed anyway. When MacNeil asked Virick if the cut could have been self-inflicted, the doctor responded, "It's possible."

The statement was contrary to what Virick had described during the preliminary inquiry. When asked then if the wound could have been self-inflicted, Virick had responded, "This point is against it."

Rosenblum immediately pounced on the inaccuracy, reciting directly from the transcript of the preliminary inquiry what Virick had said. By the time he was finished, Rosenblum managed to get Virick to concede that the wound had been more than a superficial scrape and that it had likely, at some point in the evening, bled.

When Harriss took the stand, she had the power to undo most of the Crown's theory of the crime, and when she started to testify, it appeared that she might do just that. When asked, she told the court that she and Gushue had actually been in the park one full hour before the time she told the police they had been there. Then, when MacNeil asked her if she had seen anyone else in the park, Harriss replied, "There wasn't many there."

"Now what do you mean by that? "MacNeil asked.

"Well, there wasn't a crowd of people there."

But when MacNeil finally bore down on Harriss and asked her how many people she had seen with Marshall, she took the path of least resistance and repeated her lie.

"One," she told the court.

MacNeil was the only person in the courtroom besides Harriss herself who knew just how damaging her true testimony could have been. Because Rosenblum had not seen Harriss' original statement, in which she said she had seen more than two people standing with Marshall, he didn't cross-examine Harriss on it. She did admit to Rosenblum under cross-examination that she did not know if the other person had been a man, woman or child, but it didn't matter. According to Harriss, Marshall had been in the company of only one other person when she and Gushue stopped to ask for a light.

If Harriss' testimony had nearly derailed the case, then Chant's time on the stand almost caused the Crown's case irreparable harm. The young man took his seat and started telling the court about how he had been walking through the park when he saw a man crouched in the bushes. He said he had also seen two men across the street arguing, but unlike at the preliminary inquiry, when he said he had heard profane language from the men, he told the jury he hadn't been able to hear what the men were saying. He also told the court he saw one man take something out: "I don't know what it was. He drove it towards the left side of the other fellow's stomach." During the preliminary inquiry, Chant had specifically said he saw a knife. And contrary to his preliminary-inquiry testimony, Chant told the jury he had not recognized the man who stabbed Seale.

The court broke for half an hour before Chant's testimony concluded. During the recess, Pratico approached Donald Marshall Senior in the hallway and told the accused's father point-blank, "Look, boy, that fellow in there didn't do it."

Marshall Senior reacted in a clear-headed fashion. He stopped Pratico from saying anything further and then went to find Khattar. Pratico repeated his statement to Khattar, who immediately asked someone to find the sheriff, who in turn sent for MacNeil. When MacNeil arrived, he brought with him MacIntyre, MacDonald and assistant prosecutor Louis Matheson. Once the small party had convened, Pratico again repeated his statement that Marshall was innocent.

The ensuing conversation was brief. When Pratico explained that he'd been scared when the police questioned him, both MacNeil and MacIntyre reacted as if they'd been personally offended. Khattar advised Pratico that the best thing he could do was to tell the truth. MacNeil countered by explaining just how serious the crime of perjury was under the Criminal Code of Canada. The meeting broke up shortly afterwards with no indication from Pratico as to what he would do when he took the stand.

Pratico quickly faded from the minds of all involved when court reconvened and Chant resumed his testimony. So far, the witness had managed to evade naming Marshall as the man who stabbed Seale. Despite his preliminary-inquiry testimony, Chant had told the jury that he had not recognized the man. After the recess, however, Judge Dubinsky decided to ask Chant himself exactly whom he had seen "driving" the object.

"Donald Marshall," Chant replied.

What erupted was a confusing and often exasperating question-and-answer period without the jury present. Chant's answer to Dubinsky's question went against what he had said earlier that morning, which went against what he had said in the preliminary inquiry. Chant tried to talk his way around it, saying he didn't recognize Marshall at the time of the stabbing but that he later recognized him after meeting him. Frustrated, MacNeil asked Dubinsky to declare Chant a hostile witness, which would give the Crown the right to cross-examine him about his preliminary-inquiry testimony. Dubinsky agreed, and MacNeil proceeded to take Chant through every answer he had given at the inquiry, each of which Chant agreed with. And in one of those statements, Chant said he had seen Marshall stab Seale.

Rosenblum knew he was working with a delicate situation and manoeuvred accordingly. He managed to elicit that Chant couldn't be certain that one of the men he had seen arguing was, in fact, Marshall. But Chant also told the court that the first statement he gave to the police about what happened in the park had been untrue. The result was a confusing, often-fractured portion of testimony that revealed little of what had actually happened. Rosenblum hoped it was enough to create some doubt in the minds of the jury.

Pratico's stay at the mental institution had ended only nine days ago, but no one, including the defence, knew about it. As the young man took the stand, MacNeil decided to tackle the elephant in the room head-on. Rather than try to skirt around the subject of Pratico's hallway confession, MacNeil asked him about it directly, eliciting from Pratico that he had spoken to both Khattar and Marshall Senior in the hallway. The tone of MacNeil's questioning, however, suggested that Pratico had tried to change his story outside because Marshall Senior had some-how threatened him, not because his testimony wasn't true.

Dubinsky didn't know what had happened in the hall-way, and as far as he was concerned, whatever had happened had no bearing on the trial itself.

"I have nothing before me that would warrant my listen-ing to what has been up to now your questioning," Dubinsky admonished MacNeil. "So proceed with the questioning of the events of that night."

During that questioning, Pratico reverted to the revised statement he had given to the police—that he had been behind some bushes, drinking a beer, when he saw two men arguing. Pratico told the jury that he had recognized both men, naming Seale and Marshall. He also testified that Marshall had pulled something shiny out of his pocket and "plunged it into Seale's stomach."

Khattar thought he had an opening when he started Pratico's cross-examination the next day. Because Pratico had tried to recant his statement, Khattar believed he could easily raise the issue of reasonable doubt in the minds of the jury. But between Khattar's unfocused questioning and Dubinsky's igno-rance of what had happened, the effect was less than Khattar had hoped for. Khattar managed to get Pratico to describe what he had said in the hallway the day before. But when the lawyer tried to compare it with what Pratico had said during the preliminary, which had been based on the young man's revised statement to the police, Dubinsky interrupted and excused the jury so he, Khattar and MacNeil could discuss the issue. In the end, the judge told Khattar, "Confine yourself to that one statement in the evidence in the court below if you wish to [continue your line of questioning]."

Khattar took that to mean he could ask Pratico only about whether or not he had actually made the statement, not what he had meant by it. He asked Pratico to name each person who had been privy to the recantation, but did not ask why Pratico had said it or what he had meant by it.

After the defence concluded, MacNeil stood again to ask a few more questions about issues that had emerged during the cross-examination. Those questions focused specifically on Pratico's recantation and who had heard it.

"Now why did you make that statement yesterday that Mr. Khattar referred to as being made—why did you make that statement which is inconsistent with your evidence as given before these gentlemen and his Lordship in this trial?" MacNeil asked.

"Scared," Pratico replied.

"Scared of what?" Dubinsky asked.

"Of my life being taken."

The implication was clear, if not exact—Pratico had said Marshall was innocent because he was afraid for his life. The jury was left with the impression that Marshall Senior had somehow threatened the young man.

Shortly after Pratico testified, the Crown rested its case. The defence had few options available to try to prove Marshall's innocence, and though they had tried to poke holes in the testimonies of the Crown's star witnesses, Rosenblum and Khattar weren't confident they had succeeded. They were left with only one choice—to put Marshall on the stand to explain himself.

The decision, however, proved to be a poor one. Marshall was not a co-operative witness. His voice rose barely above a whisper as he replied to questions, and he frequently covered his mouth with his hand while speaking, prompting Dubinsky to ask him repeatedly to speak up. When his answers were audible, they were short and monosyllabic, lacking any real insight.

Marshall stuck with the story he had given to the police, that he and Seale had been in the park when the two men dressed like priests came over to ask for a smoke and a light. Suddenly one of the men had declared he didn't like "Indians or niggers" and stabbed Seale.

"Did you stab Seale?" Rosenblum asked.

"No," Marshall replied.

"Or lay hands on him of any kind?"

"No."

MacNeil confronted Marshall with some evidence during his cross-examination, asking why Gushue and Harriss testified that he was alone with Seale if hadn't been. Marshall replied that he didn't remember meeting either that night, that his mind had gone blank. He swore to the jury that his arm had, in fact, been bleeding earlier in the evening and that he hadn't seen Pratico in the park at any time. The Crown's whole story, he tried to say, was false.

Marshall's testimony was all that could have saved him, but it was lacking. When Rosenblum stood to summarize his client's defence, he spoke for 43 minutes. He wondered aloud why, if all these people had seen Marshall stab Seale, no one had told the police in the park to arrest him on the spot. He wondered why Marshall had voluntarily hung around the Sydney police station for the better part of two days. Were those the actions of a guilty man?

At 12:35 PM on November 5, having charged the jury with their task, Dubinsky dismissed the 12-member panel to begin deliberations. Barely four hours later, everyone was summoned back to the courthouse to hear the verdict. It was unanimous—Marshall was guilty of second-degree murder.

The sentence was automatic. After a brief statement, in which he said he hoped the jury's decision would provide some closure for the Seale family, Dubinsky turned to Marshall and sentenced him to life in prison at Dorchester Penitentiary.

～

Marshall's murder conviction started to come unravelled within months of his trial, but no one was willing to pay attention.

On November 15, just 10 days after the trial had ended, a man named Jimmy MacNeil arrived at the Sydney police station in the company of his brother and told the police that he knew who had killed Seale. It wasn't Marshall. It was a man named Roy Ebsary, and MacNeil had been standing right next to him when it had happened. He also told MacIntyre that he had watched Ebsary wash the knife clean shortly afterwards.

After conferring with the Crown's office, the police brought Ebsary, his wife and son to the station for questioning. Ebsary's daughter, Donna, was left in the car outside while the rest of the family answered questions.

Ebsary was something of a character. He had been a merchant marine, but now cut vegetables at a local hotel. He had wild grey hair and walked with a cane. He also had a violent streak—the year before, he had been arrested in possession of a knife, allegedly on his way to stab someone. He was convicted of carrying a concealed weapon.

Ebsary admitted to the police that two men had asked him for cigarettes and money, but that he had driven them off. He denied that he had been carrying a knife that night.

Based on MacNeil's testimony, the Crown filed a request with the RCMP to review the Sydney police file on the Seale murder. Both Sergeant G.M. McKinley and Inspector E.A. Marshall were tasked with the review. They started with a polygraph test, subjecting both Ebsary and MacNeil to the so-called lie detector. In Ebsary's case, the polygraph analyst found no evidence of deception and informed the police that he didn't believe MacNeil was mentally capable of responding to the test. In the end, Inspector Marshall concluded that the events were likely a figment of MacNeil's imagination.

Neither investigator interviewed any of the witnesses again; they only reviewed the file. Their conclusions mirrored those of the investigating officer, and the matter was again filed away.

No one bothered telling Marshall or his lawyer that the review was underway. Seven months later, the Appeals Division of the Supreme Court of Nova Scotia denied Marshall's appeal.

Three years later, another witness showed up at the police station with another story to tell. In the company of her martial arts instructor, Donna Ebsary, now 17, told the police the tale that had haunted her for years. According to Donna, on the night of May 28, 1971, she had been standing on the steps in her home, about to go upstairs, when she saw her father walk in with Jimmy MacNeil. Her father hadn't noticed her, but Donna watched him pull a bloody knife from beneath his robe and begin washing it in the kitchen sink.

The police, however, weren't interested. They told Donna that the case was closed and they were too busy to investigate.

They never took a statement, and no one bothered telling the Crown.

~

A life sentence in the Canadian justice system seldom means exactly that.

Few inmates spend their entire lives behind bars. Under the Criminal Code of Canada, even people convicted of first-degree murder are eligible for parole after serving a specified minimum sentence.

But a key part in securing a parole release is admitting one's guilt, and Marshall was convinced of his innocence, even if no one else was. He admitted his guilt only once, in 1974, so he could be transferred from Dorchester Penitentiary to a medium-security institution in Springhill. Shortly after the transfer, Marshall recanted his admission.

Prison life was not easy on the young man, but he was tough enough to endure it. His endurance was fortified by drugs smuggled into the prison and by his fists, which made him one of the most feared inmates. When it came to drugs, Marshall took anything he could get his hands on, from Valium to marijuana. When it came to defending himself and his reputation, he was vicious. He was always getting into fights, but he was also winning all of them.

Despite his protestations of innocence, Marshall was far from being a model prisoner. Besides his drug use and combative nature, he found himself frequently running afoul of the prison's rules. Every parole officer who encouraged him to own up to his crime was met with the same response—total denial. This, combined with his behaviour, made Marshall an unfavourable candidate for any kind of parole. He was denied temporary passes to attend funerals and family functions. He spent several stints bound up in "the hole," the solitary confinement unit.

Marshall did make some progress behind bars. He upgraded his schooling to Grade 10, joined Alcoholics Anonymous and the Native Brotherhood. He even started training to learn to be a plumber. Eventually, Corrections relented and allowed him to attend a survival course away from the jail. On August 8, 1979, Marshall was approved for the Atlantic Challenge Canoeing trip, which would be held from September 15 to 24. He had already been allowed to attend one survival course the year before, but Marshall had bigger plans for this trip. He spent the preceding six weeks winning as much money as he could playing cards with other inmates.

On September 24, the last day of the trip, the group was driving back to the institution when the guard stopped for gas. When his back was turned, Marshall bolted for freedom.

That freedom was short-lived. Although he was able to use the skills he had learned on his survival course to stay ahead of the police and had some well-placed contacts on the outside to help him, Marshall's freedom lasted a mere two days. The police in Pictou stormed his girlfriend's house and brought him

back in. On October 18, Marshall was sentenced to another
four months in custody, consecutive to his life term, for being
unlawfully at large. One year later, the authorities transferred
Marshall from the relatively relaxed atmosphere at Springhill
back to maximum security at Dorchester.

∼

When a story needs to be told, it's difficult to stop it. The
story of Marshall's innocence, though 10 years late, eventually
came to light through a strange confluence of time, place and
circumstance. On August 26, 1981, Shelly Sarson, Marshall's
girlfriend, paid him a visit at Dorchester. Sarson's brother Mitchell tagged along for the trip, but with a more important purpose.

The previous year, Mitchell had roomed with an older
man named Roy Ebsary while he was attending school in
Sydney. Ebsary, it turned out, was a homosexual who was now
separated from his wife. One night, he had told Mitchell that he
had once stabbed a black man and a Native back in 1971.

Marshall could scarcely believe what he was hearing, but
he acted quickly. He contacted Roy Gould, the chief of the
Membertou reserve, who contacted the Union of Nova Scotia
Indians, which brought the matter to the attention of the
Sydney police. After the police reviewed the file, they contacted
the new Crown prosecutor, Frank Edwards, who asked the
RCMP to investigate again.

Staff Sergeant Harry Wheaton and Corporal Jim Carroll were tasked with conducting the review, and right from the start they felt they were on to something. Ebsary, they learned, had just been arrested for stabbing another man in Sydney. The pair met with Mitchell, who told them exactly what he had told Marshall, adding that Ebsary "had a thing about knives."

On February 16, 1982, the two officers managed to track down Chant, who had been working at a fish plant in Louisbourg and now had a child. He'd also found God after spending several years dealing drugs in Montreal. He was eager to come clean, and he told the two officers everything he'd been too afraid to mention in 1971—that he hadn't seen Marshall stab Seale, that he hadn't even been in the park when it had happened and that MacIntyre had pressured him to change his story. Two days later, Carroll and Wheaton drove out to Dorchester and interviewed Marshall. For the first time ever, Marshall finally admitted that he and Seale had been trying to rob the two men when the stabbing occurred. The detectives left without making any promises, but with a growing sense that something was not right with Marshall's conviction.

They met with Pratico the next day at a walk-in clinic in New Waterford. The young man had been diagnosed with schizophrenia and lived a transient existence. His mind, however, was still sharp. When they read Pratico the statement he had given to the police in 1971, the young man denied every single word of it, reaffirming that he hadn't been anywhere near the park that night.

Both officers felt that Sarson's description of Ebsary closely mirrored Marshall's original description of the assailant. With the evidence mounting, Carroll and Wheaton asked Ebsary to come in for an interview. When they first confronted Ebsary with their evidence, the old man denied everything. Hours later, after the police released him, he called the station and admitted to stabbing Seale. But when they brought him in the next day to extract a written confession, they found him drunk and unwilling to co-operate. He said he would confess if he could meet Marshall's parents. Carroll and Wheaton set up the meeting. Ebsary talked with the grief-stricken couple but did not confess anything.

On February 27, the police tracked down the last key witness of the Crown's case against Marshall, and she was more than happy to co-operate. Harriss told the police she had definitely seen Marshall in the park with three other men, one of whom had grey hair and was wearing a blue coat.

The icing on the cake would be physical evidence, and for that Wheaton turned to Ebsary's ex-wife, Mary. Wheaton paid a visit to Mary and her son, Greg, who mentioned that some of his father's knives were boxed up in the basement. At Wheaton's suggestion, Mary selected two knives she thought her husband might have used to stab Seale. In March, both were packaged up and sent to the lab in Halifax for testing, along with some of Roy's clothing. It had been 10 years since the stabbing; there was a slim chance of finding any evidence.

But the testing paid off. Later that month, Adolphus Evers, the man who had given testimony about clothing fibres during Marshall's trial, called with exciting news. He had found a fibre on one of the knives sent to him, and it matched a sample fibre from the jacket Seale had been wearing that night. Evers explained that he had also found three fibres on the same knife matching the jacket Marshall had been wearing.

Carroll and Wheaton contacted the Crown, which contacted the Attorney General. Within days, the National Parole Board granted Marshall full parole. On March 29, 1982, Marshall cleaned out his cell at Dorchester and finally walked away.

But he wasn't a free man yet. He was just on parole. He lived at the Carleton Centre, a halfway house, and had to observe certain conditions in order to maintain his parole. It was hard for Marshall. He was innocent but still being treated like a convict.

It took eight months, but eventually the Nova Scotia Court of Appeal opened a hearing into the matter on the advice of then Justice Minister Jean Chrétien. Witnesses who 11 years earlier had pointed an accusing finger at Marshall now recanted everything they had said. Chant and Harriss admitted they had lied on the stand, Donna Ebsary told the story of watching her father wash the murder weapon clean, and Evers told the panel about the fibres he had found. In the end, the Crown asked the court to exonerate Marshall, but argued that Marshall himself was to blame for his predicament because he had never told anyone why he and Seale had been in the park in the first place.

The court agreed. Although a five-member panel quashed the conviction, exonerating Marshall, they laid the blame for the fiasco entirely at his feet.

"By lying, he helped secure his own conviction. He misled his lawyers and presented to the jury a version of the facts he now says is false, a version that was so far-fetched as to be incapable of belief."

Two days after the court cleared Marshall's name, Ebsary was officially charged with Seale's murder. The case, however, would not be an easy one. The first trial, in September 1983, ended in a hung jury. A second jury found Ebsary guilty and sentenced him to five years, but the verdict was overturned on appeal. On January 7, 1985, a third jury found him guilty, and the judge sentenced him to three years, which was reduced to one year on appeal. Seven months later, Ebsary collapsed in his room at a Sydney rooming house and died of a heart attack.

The government couldn't ignore the comedy of errors that had led to Marshall's conviction. In 1987, the Conservatives empanelled the Royal Commission on the Donald Marshall Junior Prosecution. Three years and $8 million later, the commission published a scathing report, blasting the Sydney police, the original trial judge, former Crown prosecutor Donald MacNeil and Marshall's defence lawyer Moe Rosenblum.

"The criminal justice system failed Donald Marshall at virtually every turn, from his arrest and wrongful conviction for murder in 1971 up to and even beyond his acquittal by the Court of Appeal in 1983," the final report read.

That same year, the government of Nova Scotia formally apologized to Marshall. In the end he received $900,000 in compensation and later became a principal figure in a Supreme Court of Canada ruling on Native hunting and fishing rights.

But the ghosts of his wrongful conviction never disappeared. On January 2, 2006, Marshall was arrested and charged by the police in Nova Scotia with attempted murder for trying to run down a man with his car. A judged ordered that the case be held over until a psychiatric evaluation could be completed.

Chapter Three

Guy Paul Morin

Queensville, Ontario
April 10, 1985

S he said she was a hairdressing student, and no one doubted her. But she wasn't really anything of the sort. Constable Anne Crawford was actually a veteran police officer with 18 years of experience under her belt, but not tonight. Tonight Crawford was a cheery wannabe beautician hanging out in Queensville with the local community band. She was a friend of the bandleader's daughter, she told everyone, and no one doubted her.

Her request must have seemed strange, but apparently it wasn't strange enough to warrant questioning. It actually made her quite popular. The musicians lined up, one by one, in front of Crawford and obligingly passed a comb through their hair or plucked single strands from their scalps and placed them in envelopes. Finally, after what seemed like an eternity, a dark-haired clarinet player approached her and offered his sample.

Crawford's pulse quickened. This was the man she was after.

The clarinet player stood still as Crawford gently ran the comb through his thick dark hair. It took a few tries, but eventually she liberated a few strands. She managed a smile as the man joked about his hair and tried to flirt with her. A wave of relief passed over her as soon as he walked away.

After staying long enough to keep up the pretence of her visit, Crawford raced away from the band practice to meet up with two other police officers. She passed one envelope over to the pair, who thanked her for her efforts and left.

The next morning, the same two detectives marched into the Centre for Forensic Sciences (CFS) in Toronto and personally presented Stephanie Nyznyk with the sample. She took the envelope, removed a strand of hair and placed it under a microscope. When she looked up, she smiled.

"Congratulations, gentlemen," Nyznyk said. "They are consistent with coming from the same source as the necklace hair."

Little did Nyznyk know just how powerful her words would be. Twelve days later, a squad of police officers descended on a gold Honda stopped at a red light in Queensville and arrested the driver, 24-year-old Guy Paul Morin, for the rape and murder of Christine Jessop.

It turned out that their case against Morin was as thin as the hair on which it was founded, but no one would acknowledge that for years to come.

~

To this day, no one knows what actually happened to Christine Jessop after 4:00 PM on October 3, 1984.

The school bus dropped the nine-year-old off outside her home sometime around 3:45 PM. At the time she had in her possession a brand new musical instrument—a recorder—complete with a strip of tape on it bearing her name.

Around 4:00, Jessop went to the nearby general store and purchased a piece of gum. She was seen outside the store shortly afterwards, talking with a group of boys. A witness who later recanted her testimony told the police she saw Jessop pushing her bike back up the driveway.

No one ever saw her alive again.

Jessop was supposed to meet one of her friends at the nearby park, but she never showed up. Her mother, Janet, and brother, Ken, returned home sometime between 4:10 and 4:35 from Ken's dental appointment. They found Christine's bike lying on its side in the shed, her jacket hung on a peg inside the house and her backpack on the pantry counter. They also found the mail and the newspaper inside.

It took several hours for Janet to realize something was wrong. She thought Christine was probably at the park, but by

7:00, with no sign of Christine, Janet began to worry. She placed a call to the York Regional Police and reported her daughter missing.

The first officer to arrive at the Jessop home took a quick statement from Janet and then quickly called for backup. As word of the girl's disappearance filtered through the tiny community, more and more volunteers showed up at the house to search for Christine. The volunteer fire department mobilized, and a local police officer who had a private interest in training search dogs joined the hunt. The searchers fanned out through the community, knocking on doors and beating bushes, calling out the girl's name.

One family that did not bother turning up to help in the search was the Jessops' next-door neighbours. Alphonse and Ida Morin, along with their 24-year-old live-in son, Guy Paul, were generally seen as outcasts in the community. Their house was in shambles, seemingly caught in a storm of renovations that were never completed. The interior of the house was crammed with boxes and bags of knick-knacks. They were a handy family, but seemed interested only in working on their many cars once the sun had gone down.

One officer approached the Morin residence and asked Alphonse to let him in to search inside for Christine. Alphonse refused.

Outside the Morin house, Constable David Robertson passed an article of Christine's clothing beneath the snout of his dog Ryder. After making sure the dog had gotten a good whiff of the clothing, Robertson turned him loose. Ryder immediately ran up to the gold Honda parked on the Morins' property, began sniffing pronouncedly and then reared up and placed his front paws on the window of the car. Robertson didn't bother telling anyone and didn't make a note of the incident. He and Ryder continued on with their search for Christine.

Approximately 60 kilometres away, three pairs of ears suddenly perked up in different homes. The residents tried to place the sound they were hearing—it sounded like a girl screaming. They waited for the sound to repeat itself, but it never did. No one bothered investigating.

It was not until the sun began to rise the following morning, with no sign of Jessop, that the York Regional Police began to suspect she might be more than just missing. Because they hadn't suspected foul play, they had failed to initiate some fairly standard procedures. No one had sealed off the Jessop household or Christine's bedroom as a potential crime scene. No one had dusted the interior of the home for fingerprints.

Based on the careless position of Christine's bike and the fact that her jacket had been hung on a hook that was out of her reach, the police assumed she had been kidnapped from inside the Jessop home. Yet there were no signs of forced entry. Janet and Ken, who was actually adopted, hadn't returned home until after Christine had disappeared. Christine's father, Bob, was locked up in jail, serving an 18-month sentence for trying to defraud a senior-citizen couple by convincing them to grant him power of attorney. Christine was a typical nine-year-old girl, the police assumed—loveable and sweet with no enemies.

At the time of Jessop's abduction, there were 140 known sex offenders living in the area. Investigators began searching for all of them, but each one seemed to have an alibi for the night of October 3. The police had nothing to go on. Even though there were 1,000 volunteers combing the surrounding area, no one had turned up any clues or an eyewitness who could give them some place to start. All they could do was sit and wait.

The police got some leads as they worked, but none amounted to anything significant. The Morins' daughter, Yvette Devine, told an officer she had been at her parents' home on October 3 and saw a white car parked in the Jessops' driveway. She could not, however, provide a good description of who had been in the car. Her brother, Guy Paul, was of even less help to the police than Yvette. One day in November when the police were again conducting a door-to-door search, they asked Guy Paul if they could speak to him in their car. He told the officers he knew nothing about Jessop's disappearance. When the officers asked Morin for his parents' phone number to follow up with him in the future, he refused to give it to them.

As November rolled into December, the people in Queensville were beginning to get upset with the police. The town of Queensville was small and children seldom disappeared. The York Regional Police had followed up on a few leads, questioning one man whose wife claimed he was a sexual sadist and had raped her daughter. The man told the police he had spent October 3 at home, making preserves. No one else had been with him. Despite their efforts, none of the investigators could link him to Jessop's disappearance.

On the final day of 1984, a man named Fred Patterson noticed some dogs rustling around in the bush on his property, 50 kilometres away from Queensville on Rural Route 2. Patterson and his daughter went over to investigate. Minutes later, the police received a frantic phone call.

The members of the Durham Regional Police who responded to the call had a pretty good idea whose remains they would find when they responded to the call. The body of a young girl—what was left of it—was lying flat on the ground, her legs spread in an unnatural position. While the legs were still fleshy, most of the upper torso had decomposed to bone. The skeleton was wearing only socks, and a ball of blue clothing sat on the ground nearby. There was a pair of girls' panties next to the corpse, as well as a running shoe.

Sergeant Michael Michalowsky, head of the Durham Regional Police Identification Branch, arrived on scene at

2:00 PM, one hour after the body had been found. While preservation of the scene should have been the first thing on his mind, Michalowsky was more concerned about the weather. There was supposed to be a snowstorm moving into the area, and he was sure the snow would blanket the scene, covering up any evidence. He rejected the suggestion of one officer that they erect a tarp over the body and instead tasked the officers on scene to begin searching the area for other evidence.

Most police searches of a crime scene, especially with a body involved, are systematic. Police officers divide the area into square grids using string and diligently search every square in the grid, making notes on each one as they go. Michalowsky, however, didn't bother with a grid search, instead ordering his team to form a line and search the area.

A few metres away, Constable Tom Cameron extinguished a cigarette on the bottom of his boot and flicked the butt into the grass nearby. Officers later photographed one, possibly two cigarette butts at the scene.

According to Kirk Makin's book *Redrum the Innocent*, the search of the area was far from perfect. Besides the haste with which it was conducted and the failure to use proper, proven search techniques, the treatment of Jessop's remains led to a lack of forensic evidence available later to the team. While Michalowsky took some soil samples from the area with the hope that they might yield traces of blood or bodily fluids, the way in which Jessop's body was removed may have contaminated the crime scene. After loosening the soil around the body, a group of police officers slid a plywood sheet beneath it. They did not dig a larger hole around the corpse to further analyze the soil on which the body had been lying, and they did not remove the soil directly beneath the body for testing. The threat of an impending snowstorm tainted the entire search by pushing Michalowsky and his team to work faster and less carefully than they normally would have. The team was also unaccustomed to working murder scenes.

Jessop's body arrived at the coroner's office at about 8:00 that night. A cursory inspection of the body yielded one important clue right away: the technicians removed from a gold chain around Jessop's neck a single dark hair that did not match her own. The hair was bagged and sent to the CFS for further analysis.

John Hillsdon Smith, the chief pathologist for Ontario, arrived on the morning of January 2 to conduct the autopsy. But the initial indications of the cause of Jessop's death proved confusing, and Smith started to wonder if the body had somehow been contaminated. Samples of Jessop's bone marrow had been removed and sent for a diatom test, in which the marrow is tested for the presence of micro-organisms, or diatoms. The diatoms enter the body in drowning cases when water enters the bloodstream through the lungs.

The diatom test came back positive, which could indicate that Jessop had drowned. Although Smith believed the sample might have been contaminated, he came across another sign pointing to drowning. When he examined Jessop's skull, which was found apart from her body, he found pink stains on her teeth, also an indication of drowning. The skull revealed further clues. Smith noted two fractures, which indicated that whoever killed Jessop had struck her at least twice in the head sharply and quickly. He concluded that Jessop had been alive at the time of injury.

Smith also noticed two holes in the remaining skin on Jessop's upper torso. Looking more closely at the ribs, he saw several nick marks a few millimetres in depth that had obviously been inflicted with a sharp knife. They corresponded with several bloodstained holes found in the clothing recovered at the body site. Jessop's clothing was missing several buttons, but Michalowsky claimed all of the buttons had been recovered. It was later revealed that only two buttons had been found.

In the end, Smith ruled the cause of death as stabbing and said he believed Jessop had been sexually assaulted. Analysts found a semen stain on the inside of her underwear, which raised a new possibility. If Jessop had been sexually assaulted, she had likely put her clothing back on at some point, which suggested that she had likely been sexually assaulted, and possibly killed, somewhere else. Other evidence was pointing to that theory as well. There was a remarkable lack of blood found in the soil around her body, indicating she could have been killed somewhere else and dumped where she had been found. Rather than dub that area the "crime scene," the police began referring to it as the body site.

Between January 2 and 4, the police returned to the site with propane heaters and melted down the recently accumulated snow to continue the search for clues. They turned up a few curious items, such as a cigarette lighter, some nails and garbage, but the most intriguing find turned out to be a small set of bones, including a rib and a vertebra, that were sent off for testing.

The Durham Regional Police, who now had jurisdiction over Jessop's case because her body was found in their territory, interviewed three of the families who lived near the body site. At one household, a woman named Lydia Robertson claimed she had heard screams coming from somewhere in the area one night in October. She told the police she had heard a female voice screaming, "Help, help, please don't," repeatedly. When she had discussed it with her son Alex, they agreed it must have been some guy beating his wife and didn't bother investigating.

When interviewed by the police, two other residents in the area didn't recall hearing anything suspicious, but both later contacted investigators to tell them that they had, in fact, heard some sort of screaming.

Even with Jessop's body now in their possession, investigators had few leads to go on. Detectives Bernie Fitzpatrick and

John Shephard had been assigned to the case. They looked again at the man who had been brought to their attention earlier, whose wife had alerted the police and who claimed he had been making preserves on the day Jessop disappeared. They put him under surveillance and obtained a search warrant for his home, but found nothing incriminating. He even agreed to a polygraph test and passed it. He was dismissed as a suspect.

~

On January 7, Jessop's remains were laid to rest in Queensville. Bob Jessop had been let out of prison on compassionate grounds when his daughter had disappeared, and he and Janet hosted a small reception on the evening after the funeral. As the guests sat in the living room and chatted, a pair suddenly shushed the rest of the group, asking them to listen. Everyone strained their ears but heard nothing.

Three or four people, however, would claim that they had. They later told the police that they had clearly heard someone outside screaming the words "God help me!" Janet initially denied she had heard anything, but that would change, as would other parts of her testimony, as the investigation unfolded.

~

The police had hundreds of tips to follow up on in Jessop's death, but none were amounting to anything substantial. One man claimed he had seen a man in the area of the body site who disappeared into the bush carrying an axe and a pick.

Another talked about seeing a vehicle parked in the area with its trunk up. When the witness stopped to see if the man needed help, the man just slammed the trunk of his vehicle closed and gave him an evil stare.

The police received a tip about a young man with a history of sexual misconduct and violence. He had once threatened to kill a teacher. Though he was initially cleared by the York police, Fitzpatrick and Shephard decided to investigate the teen. The young man had worked at the cemetery behind the Jessop and Morin houses, but his family claimed their son had been with them on the night Jessop disappeared. The police considered it a strong alibi.

Both Fitzpatrick and Shephard continued to interview the Jessops, hoping that something would eventually come to light. Although Janet's story occasionally changed, it did not provide any substantial clues. She had adjusted the time she thought she and Ken had arrived home on October 3, now saying it could have been between 4:20 and 4:35 PM. Ken agreed. In an interview on February 14, Janet made an off-hand comment that the detectives noted in their books and triggered a decade-long sequence of events.

"Guy Paul Morin. Weird-type guy."

With that in mind, and with no better suspects, the pair decided it was time to start paying more attention to this "weird" young man who lived next door. Within days, though they lacked any tangible evidence, the detectives were already treating

Morin more seriously as a suspect. One even made a note in a notebook referring to Morin as "the suspect."

Morin could have been considered weird because he didn't fit the stereotype of a 24-year-old man. He did not spend his spare time playing hockey, driving trucks, drinking heavily and having sex. He lived at home with his parents and spent his spare time working on his cars or helping out with repairs around the house. He kept beehives in the area out behind the Morin household. He worked as a finishing sander for a Toronto furniture manufacturer and in his spare time played the clarinet in a local band.

On February 22, Fitzpatrick and Shephard arrived at the Morin house and invited the young man to join them in their police cruiser for a chat. Unbeknownst to Morin, the detectives had a hidden tape recorder turning away inside the car.

The most important piece of information they gained was probably the one the detectives ended up ignoring. As the three got comfortable, Fitzpatrick asked Morin if he smoked. Morin replied that he didn't. The detectives noted Morin's response in their books and promptly forgot about it.

Though Morin spent 90 minutes inside the detectives' car, the most incriminating statements Morin is alleged to have made weren't captured on tape. For some reason, the recorder stopped about halfway through the interview. The detectives later claimed they thought the tape recorder would automatically reverse when the first side of the 90-minute tape came to an end. Regardless of what happened, the recorder stopped and the two officers had to rely on their memories of what Morin said.

What Morin told them was suspect in some ways. In talking about the case in general, Morin, as he was sometimes want to do, let his mind run wild, putting most of his thoughts to voice. One of them in particular stuck out in the minds of the officers. Though it wasn't recorded on tape, both officers alleged that Morin made a statement to the effect that "all little girls are sweet and beautiful, but they grow up to be corrupt."

Morin answered a few questions, saying he never really talked to Jessop. He never hugged her, never played with her or played his clarinet for her. He told the pair that he'd returned home from working in Toronto at around 4:30 PM on the day of Jessop's disappearance. He also told the detectives that when he and his father had observed the police gathering at the Jessop household the same day, he told his father, "I bet that little Christine is gone."

Fitzpatrick and Shephard asked Morin if he would take a polygraph test. He said he would if it was necessary, but that he would prefer not to. At the end of the interview, Morin returned to his home, and the detectives started wondering what else they could learn about their suspect.

They started with a trip to Morin's employer in Toronto, where they obtained his time card for October 3. It showed that Morin had, in fact, punched out at 3:32 PM that day. The detectives clocked the trip from Morin's place of work to the Jessop home to see if he could have returned with enough time to kidnap Jessop. They made the trip in approximately 42 minutes, putting Morin home at around 4:15.

The timing was becoming critical. The statements of the staff at the dental clinic where Janet and Ken had been that day were proving to be important as well. The dentist and a receptionist at the office both said that Janet had picked Ken up from the office sometime between 4:20 and 4:30. It was close, but based on what they had learned to date, including Janet's revised arrival time, Morin could have returned home in enough time to kidnap Jessop. The detectives interviewed the Jessops again, who now said they had returned home at around 4:35.

Fitzpatrick and Shephard now turned to Stephanie Nyznyk, who was an analyst at the CFS, to help them bolster their case. Nyznyk was responsible for examining the trace evidence found at the body site. She had secured and looked at the hair found in Jessop's necklace and determined that it did not belong to the little girl. She had sent three small plastic chips from the scene to the chemistry section for analysis, but the chips disappeared. She had verified the presence of semen on the inside of Jessop's underpants and examined the soil found on the bottom of the little girl's shoes. The samples were consistent with the dirt found at the body site, meaning Jessop could have walked into the site where her body was found.

The pair of detectives also solicited the help of a high-profile figure in the world of criminal behaviour. John Douglas was the head of the FBI Centre for the Analysis of Violent Crime, the division responsible for the pseudo-science of criminal profiling. Douglas was one of the early pioneers of profiling, a practice in which investigators examined different factors such as the nature of the crime, the crime scene and other data to gain insight into what kind of person the killer might be and how he or she might behave.

It turned out that Douglas was going to be in Canada on an unrelated case, and he volunteered to help Fitzpatrick and Shephard out. They took the FBI agent on a tour of Queensville and gave him access to all of the information they had accumulated to date. The profile Douglas produced didn't clearly match the detectives' key suspect, Morin. According to Douglas, the frenzied nature of the stab wounds suggested that the killer was either a woman, or a man drunk or on drugs. It was likely, Douglas concluded, that the kidnapper hadn't intended to kill Jessop, but had stabbed her because Jessop grew uncooperative. The killer likely would have been splattered in blood and would have had to clean up afterwards. His or her behaviour after the crime would have been very stiff and nervous. The killer was likely in his or her late teens or early twenties and lived a "lifetime of failure and battered self-perception." He or she possibly had a visible handicap and might have had a criminal record for charges such as arson, breaking and entering, and voyeurism.

Jessop, Douglas theorized, had probably been excited about her new recorder and, with no one home when she got back from school, went looking for someone to show it to. At the time, the suspect was probably in a stressed and agitated state. He or she likely had a job involving manual labour and preferred working night shifts.

Douglas suggested that the detectives should use the press to help drive the killer out into the open. They should give interviews to the media, talk about new policing and investigative techniques they were using and emphasize that they would never give up. When they arrested a suspect, they should decorate the interrogation room with posters, evidence and other props to give the impression they had established some sort of Christine Jessop task force. During questioning, they should act sympathetic and tell the suspect that Jessop had been wrong to seduce or lead the suspect on.

On March 14, Global Television aired a news broadcast devoted entirely to Jessop's murder. Janet took part in the exercise, playing herself in the re-enactment. Although the program generated a new storm of tips, the police followed them up only on a cursory basis. They thought they had their man, and they were ready to pounce.

On April 10, Constable Anne Crawford went under cover to Morin's band practice. She posed as a friend of the bandleader's daughter and told everyone she was studying esthetics. She went around asking for hair samples and collected some to keep her story believable. The only hair sample she really wanted, though, was Morin's. Given his friendly nature, it was only a matter of time before Morin approached Crawford and offered himself up for a sample.

Fitzpatrick and Shephard took the hair to Nyznyk's office at the CFS. Nyznyk compared Morin's hair with the one found caught in Jessop's necklace and informed the detectives that Morin's hair was consistent with the hair from the necklace.

Buoyed by the news, the detectives secured a search warrant for Morin's gold Honda and descended on it while he was at band practice. They used adhesive tapes to extract trace and fibre samples from the car's interior, praying that if Jessop had been in the car, she had left something of herself or her clothing behind.

Shephard then spoke at a press conference, releasing selected parts of Douglas' profile to the media. The parts he released, such as the likely age and nocturnal habits of the killer and the killer's generally unkempt nature, pointed almost directly at Morin. He also told the press about Douglas' theory that the killer never meant to harm Jessop, but had lost control of her.

Two days later, Nyznyk called the detectives to tell them she had managed to match some fibres from Jessop's corpse to fibres found in Morin's Honda. It was the slam dunk the detectives were hoping for. On April 23, they obtained both an arrest warrant for Morin and a search warrant for his home. They waited until 7:45 that night, when Morin was driving to band practice, to move in on him. With 14 officers watching, Shephard pulled

Morin over to the side of the road and informed him that he was under arrest for the murder of Jessop.

∽

The entire trip to the Whitby police station was filled with Morin's proclamations of innocence, but Fitzpatrick and Shephard weren't listening. After processing their suspect, they placed him in the interrogation room.

The detectives had followed Douglas' instructions to the letter. The room was covered in posters and flowcharts. One very large blow-up poster of a fingerprint dominated the room. Morin, however, was not intimidated. He handed over the small pocketknife he always carried and willingly provided hair and saliva samples. After admitting to nothing during questioning, he was placed in solitary confinement—"the hole"—for his own safety.

The officers who searched the Morin house found nothing incriminating. There was no blood, no bloody knife and no sign of the blue knitted sweater that Jessop had supposedly been wearing the night she disappeared and that the police had yet to recover. Although they left the Morin house with boxes full of evidence, none of it was found to contain any blood. The only bloodstains found were three tiny drops inside Morin's Honda that were too small for analysis. Three hairs, believed to match Jessop's, were found in the Honda. Furthermore, the RCMP Crime Lab in Ottawa, having examined the necklace hair, announced that it was 4,500 times more likely to have come from Morin than from anyone else.

The evidence, however, was still circumstantial. The police needed some sort of eyewitness testimony, so they decided to try the undercover route again. Constable Gordon Hobbs of the Toronto Metropolitan Police was sent into jail and lodged in the same cell as Morin, wired for sound recording, in the hopes that Morin would confess to him. The resulting recordings, however, were of poor quality, and Morin never did admit he had killed Jessop, but he did make a few eyebrow-raising comments. At one point, when Hobbs asked Morin what he did when he was frustrated, Morin replied "Me, I just redrum the innocent. That's my cure, you know man, like you."

The reference was to one of Morin's favourite movies, *The Shining*. Redrum is "murder" spelled backwards. Morin repeated the word over and over again, trying to explain the gist of the movie to Hobbs, who took Morin's statement to mean something else entirely. Hobbs also noted another comment Morin made about Jessop—"No one knows the real relationship we had."

Hobbs eventually asked to be relieved of his duties, claiming that Morin's redrum reference had frightened him to the point that he was concerned for his own safety. The Crown, however, was satisfied with both the recordings that Hobbs had obtained and his written notes.

There was one hitch in the case that developed unexpect-
edly. One day, Bob, Janet and Ken visited the body site where
Christine's body had been found. During their time there, they
came across a small pile of bones later found to be human. The
pile contained a rib, a finger bone and three pieces of a shattered
vertebra. They alerted the police, who sent the bones to the CFS
for analysis. After being identified as human, they were shipped
back to the Durham police. Morin's defence team wouldn't
learn of them for years.

Morin's preliminary hearing was nothing more than
a formality, and Judge Norman Edmonson ordered Morin
bound over for trial. After the preliminary, the Morins fired
Guy Paul's first lawyer, Alex Sosna, and hired Clayton Ruby in
his place.

The police were still hard at work trying to cement the
case against Morin, even if that meant relying on some fairly
disreputable characters to do so. Shortly after Hobbs had finished his undercover duty, a convicted criminal named Robert
Dean May, serving time for petty fraud and cheque forgery, was
lodged in the same cell as Morin. Another man, a convicted sex
offender jailed for assaulting an older women and two children,
was placed in the cell next door. The man's name is still covered
by a publication ban, and he has been referred to in literature
only as Mr. X.

On July 1, both May and Mr. X asked to meet with the
detectives investigating Morin's case. Shephard attended, along

with Detective Doug King. May informed the pair that Morin had broken down in front of him the night before and started crying. May said that during the breakdown, Morin had stated, "I killed her. I killed that girl." Mr. X told the detectives that he had overheard the conversation from his cell next door.

When May returned to his cell, he did so wearing a wire. When he tried to engage Morin in conversation about the day of October 3, Morin responded with a detailed account of how he had spent his day: he had left work and stopped at a lottery booth, three grocery stores and a gas station before heading home. It was the best May could do, but the detectives were still happy to have both him and Mr. X testify at Morin's trial. In exchange, the detectives said they would see what they could do about the men's respective sentences.

Some of the physical evidence and testing procedures were turning out to be suspect. The staff at the CFS had not been able to match the soil in Morin's Honda with the soil found on Jessop's remains. Although the police had gathered 150 hairs from other people, mostly schoolchildren, in Queensville to try to match with the necklace hair, the hairs had never actually been examined. Nyznyk had found red animal fibres, similar to wool, on many of the samples she examined from Jessop, but found none inside the Honda. It was later revealed that one of the CFS lab technicians often wore red wool sweaters to work and refused to wear a lab coat. Furthermore, few of the fibres from Jessop's clothes matched those found in Honda. Of the fibres that did match, Nyznyk could not discern their actual source.

There was also the issue of a cigarette butt found at the body site. One of Ruby's assistants, while going through the list of evidence supplied by the police, found a reference to a photo of a cigarette butt that hadn't been included in the copy of the Crown's disclosure that Ruby had received. She immediately demanded a copy of the photo.

The police had also decided to engage in a questionable scientific experiment of their own. They wanted to know if it was possible that the three people living near the body site could have heard someone screaming on the night of October 3. Detective King took his two daughters down to the site, walked over to one of the houses and had the girls scream. He could barely hear them. He didn't seem to notice that it was rush hour at the time, which hadn't been the case on the night Jessop disappeared.

Ruby felt he was going to need more to work with in order to keep his client out of jail, so he explained one day to Morin the idea of a bifurcated trial. Such a trial would be split into two parts. In the first part, the jury would decide whether or not Morin had killed Jessop. If they decided he had, they would then have to decide whether or not he had done so with willful intent. Ruby wanted to raise the possibility in the jury's minds that Morin was insane at the time of the killing.

Morin hated the idea of having his sanity questioned but agreed to submit to examination by a pair of psychologists. Both concluded that Morin was, in fact, mentally ill, likely suffering from some form of schizophrenia. They believed that he could have been in a delusional state and killed Jessop without knowing it.

Trial Justice Archibald McLeod Craig granted Ruby's application for a change of venue based on the argument that everyone in the area around Queensville knew too much about the case, which would taint a jury pool selected from the area.

The trial began on January 7, 1986, and lasted for weeks. The first few Crown witnesses to take the stand were technical experts who described the state in which Jessop's body had been found, as well as the results of the autopsy and the presence of a semen stain. The first important witness was Janet Jessop, who told the jury she thought she had arrived home around 4:10 or 4:15 PM on October 3, 1984, but wasn't really sure. All she remembered for certain was that she had placed a phone call to her lawyer at 4:50. The Crown was working from the theory that Jessop had been killed immediately after her abduction and that Morin had hurried back to buy groceries and be home when the police came calling.

Prosecutor John Scott even called one of the members of Morin's band to the stand, who testified that, when she had asked Morin about the Jessop case, he had replied in a way that gave her "the creeps."

As much as the Crown hoped it would, the issue of the cigarette butt wouldn't go away. The Crown had already submitted that one of its officers, Constable Cameron, had butted out a cigarette near the body site. While cross-examining Shepherd, Ruby asked him if he would go out that evening and buy a pack of Craven A Menthols, the brand Cameron claimed to smoke. When Shephard returned with the cigarettes the next morning, Ruby asked him to describe the butt of a Craven A Menthol and compare it to the cigarette butt submitted as evidence. The two were clearly different.

"Do you agree with me from examining the cigarette butt that it could not be a Craven A Menthol?" Ruby asked.

"It does not appear to be," Shephard replied.

Ruby also pointed out that in the first transcript he received of Shephard and Fitzpatrick's February 22 interview with Morin, the question "Do you smoke?" had been deleted from the transcript. He'd made the discovery after getting his hands on another copy of the transcript. The implication was clear—Ruby was arguing that the police had tried to eliminate the butt as evidence because it could exonerate Morin, but when the police learned of a butt found at the scene, they had tried to say it was put there by one of their own officers.

Ruby also took aim at the fibre evidence submitted by Nyznyk. The issue of the necklace hair in particular provoked some questions. On cross-examination, Nyznyk admitted that the necklace hair, though similar in some respects to Morin's hair, was quite different. Morin's hair had a yellow hue that was absent in the necklace hair. Nyznyk also admitted that of all the fibres recovered from Morin's home and car, only five fibres from the car had matched fibres on Jessop's body, and those five could have gotten into the car through some kind of contamination, such as the Jessops and the Morins using the same laundromat, which they did.

The Crown's next witness was Hobbs, the Toronto police officer who had gone under cover to try to solicit a confession from Morin in jail. The results of his exercise had been questionable. Only 60 per cent of the tape recordings were decipherable, but it wasn't the tapes Ruby was concerned about. It was Hobbs' own recollections, including the redrum incident and a series of stabbing motions Hobbs said Morin had made shortly after saying, "Nobody knows the real relationship we had." Hobbs told the court that in one of the many moments not captured on tape, Morin had leaned in and asked him, "How was yours?"

"He made a stabbing motion toward the chest," Hobbs said. "He began to stab quickly and rapidly on his chest. The best I could say is half a dozen would be the closest."

Ruby confronted Hobbs directly, pointing out that the most incriminating moments were the ones not heard on tape and that no one except Hobbs could substantiate his testimony, including the stabbing motions. When asked why he didn't just asked Morin if he'd killed Jessop, Hobbs responded that he didn't want to put words in Morin's mouth.

Both May and Mr. X followed in a woeful attempt to bolster the Crown's case. Although both repeated their stories as promised, Ruby effectively countered them with arguments of his own. He pointed out their criminal records to the jury and read from a transcript in which Mr. X asked for some sort of special treatment, such as a transfer to a halfway house, in exchange for his testimony.

The Crown rested its case. It was at this point in the trial that Ruby petitioned Craig for a bifurcated trial. His petition was subsequently denied. Although the case seemed to be going well for Morin, Ruby announced that he would be submitting evidence for a defence of insanity.

On January 27, Morin stood up and took the stand.

"Did you kill Christine Jessop?" Ruby asked.

"I did not kill Christine Jessop," Morin replied.

Ruby used Morin's time on the stand to have Morin try to clear up some of the more incriminating parts of the Crown's case. Morin told the jury that he had not returned home on October 3 until after 5:00 PM because he had stopped at several grocery stores. He tried to explain that his redrum comment had been meant sarcastically, part of a game he and Hobbs had played. In response to the comment that "all little girls are sweet and beautiful, but they grow up to be corrupt," Morin said that he didn't mean all little girls, just some.

On cross-examination, Scott came right out and asked Morin why he hadn't helped search for Jessop, to which Morin responded that he worked during the day and didn't see any point in searching in the dark.

"You knew she was dead," Scott accused him.

"No, I did not know she was dead. I had no idea of such. That is an accusation."

He insisted that May and Mr. X were lying in their testimonies, admitting that he had broken down in front of May but that he never confessed to anything. In the end, Scott didn't do any visible damage to Morin's testimony, and Morin probably helped more than hindered his own case.

Yet Ruby decided to go ahead with the insanity defence. It was a questionable move. While he was still trying to argue that Morin hadn't killed Jessop, he was now asking the jury to consider that if Morin had, he hadn't been legally sane at the time. Two psychologists took the stand, both stating that Morin suffered from some form of schizophrenia, though they disagreed on the exact diagnosis. But both agreed that if Morin had killed Jessop—and they weren't saying that he had—he probably had been in an acute psychotic state at the time and likely didn't remember what he had done. A Crown psychologist agreed that Morin was likely mentally ill but not to the extent the defence experts were suggesting.

It was the last kick at establishing Morin's innocence. With no more witnesses to call, Ruby began a two-hour summation for the jury, detailing the extent of Morin's defence. He started with the insanity evidence and then worked his way through the forensic evidence, the testimonies from the under-cover officer and the two inmates, and the cigarette butt, shredding the Crown's case.

"He is different, he lives next door, he is mentally ill, but he is not guilty," Ruby concluded.

In his rebuttal, Scott wondered aloud that "it's always amazing that [psychotic breaks] occur up a wooded lane that can't be seen from the road. Astonishing. Astonishing." He asked the jury to rely on the evidence the defence had been presented, including the jailhouse testimony.

In his charge to the jury, Craig informed them that they had five choices: Morin could be guilty of first-degree murder, second-degree murder or manslaughter, or he could be found not guilty or not guilty by reason of insanity.

On February 7, 1986, after 13 hours of deliberation, the jury came back with a stunning verdict. Morin was not guilty. They had entirely rejected both the Crown's case and the insanity defence.

Unfortunately for Morin, the case did not end there.

The Crown could have lived with a verdict of not guilty by insanity, but they could not accept the actual verdict. The office of the Attorney General examined the trial transcripts to see if they could appeal the verdict. They found two possibilities—that Craig had erred when instructing the jury on the concept of reasonable doubt and that he had given improper weight to the psychiatric evidence. In the end, the Ontario Court of Appeal agreed and ordered a new trial. Morin dutifully turned himself back in and was granted bail on a $40,000 bond. He appealed to the Supreme Court of Canada, but they upheld the Court of Appeal's decision.

Ruby backed away from the case, deciding that Morin needed a lawyer with a fresh perspective. He recommended attorney Jack Pinkofsky to replace him for Morin's next trial. Pinkofsky was an exhaustive researcher for whom no piece of evidence was too small or insignificant.

That particular quirk of Pinkofsky's delayed the start of Morin's second trial by several months because Pinkofsky and his team had found disturbing information about some of the evidence the police and Crown had collected but never shared with the defence.

It turned out that the CFS hadn't bothered testing the 150 hair samples collected to compare to the necklace hair. When Pinkofsky asked them to do so, the CFS concluded that two of Jessop's classmates had hair that closely matched the necklace hair. They learned about the pile of bones the Jessops had found, which had been sent for analysis and were confirmed as being from a 12-year-old girl or boy. The original pathologist admitted he had not taken a total inventory of Christine's bones. The other small pile found with Jessop's body had been buried with her remains. They learned that the family who had vouched for the whereabouts of the young man the police had investigated briefly as a suspect might have been lying.

The Crown never told the defence about Bridget Dew, a young girl who claimed she saw Jessop in the cemetery behind the Jessop house at around 5:30 PM on October 3, 1984, talking with a boy and a girl. The defence also discovered that the police had tapped the Jessops' phone line, but destroyed all the tapes of the phone calls. What remained were written logs of each call, noting the date, time and a brief description of the call.

On March 14, 1990, the prosecution learned through a meeting with the police that Sergeant Michalowsky actually had two different notebooks about the case: an original version and a revised version. The revised version contained some notes not found in the original, and some notes from the original were missing entirely in the revised version. They shared the information with the defence. Michalowsky had used the second, newer notebook at trial. A search of his house turned up a credit card receipt found at the scene that hadn't been photographed or mentioned. A milk carton mentioned in the second notebook had not been noted in the first, and the carton had been thrown away. The first notebook claimed that all of the buttons from Jessop's clothing had been found, when in fact only two had been found that night.

Further investigation of Michalowsky revealed more disturbing behaviour. Most of the measurements he had taken at the scene were determined to be incorrect. Samples of tree leaves taken from Jessop's shoes had never been sent to the CFS and were later found in Michalowsky's house, along with 35 crime scene photos. Soil samples Michalowsky claimed he had sent to the CFS in January 1985 didn't arrive until one year later. There was no comprehensive list of exhibits, and no logs of photos taken, interviews taped or people who had handled evidence.

Michalowsky was later arrested and charged with perjury and obstruction of justice. Pinkofsky took the newly unearthed evidence and allegations before a judge for a hearing that he hoped would result in a dismissal of the charges against Morin. What followed, starting in 1990, was a one and a half year long hearing in which 109 witnesses were called to testify. More previously untendered evidence emerged. The defence learned of a police suspect, an orphan who had lived in a group home near the body site and sexually experimented with other children in the home. He had later found work as a driver hauling auto parts. On the day Jessop disappeared, the man was supposed to deliver some parts to Mississauga, but they never arrived. His boss had later tracked him down in Sharon. One day, the man had washed down the interior of his grease-covered van with powerful detergent, even though he had never cleaned it previously. A few weeks later, he had smashed the van in an accident and never called the police. In the end, he had disappeared from work without ever picking up his last paycheque. He was also known to carry a knife, but he denied kidnapping and killing Jessop.

On October 30, 1990, Jessop's little corpse was exhumed and re-examined. The results were shocking. Blatant injuries to the girl's body had not been recorded during the first autopsy. There was a gigantic cut through her breastbone. Vertebrae had been purposely cut through. The most obvious evidence that had been overlooked was the substantial damage to the facial bones of Jessop's skull. Pathologist John Ferris concluded that the attempt at dismemberment would have taken at least 30 minutes, and the killer would have been soaked in blood. Given the short time frame established, it seemed hard to believe that Morin could have kidnapped Jessop, raped her, killed her, dismembered her, cleaned himself off and been home by 5:30 PM.

The findings didn't stop there. The lack of both insect activity and blood in the soil indicated that Jessop had likely been killed elsewhere and dumped at the body site. Her internal organs were missing, but no one could say why. Decomposition fluid was found on her clothes, even though she had been found naked.

In the end, Justice James Donnelly ruled that the Crown should have told the defence about some of the evidence, but that Morin should still stand trial.

What followed was to date the longest murder trial in Canadian history. A jury of six men and six women was empanelled on November 13, 1991, to spend what would be the next nine months of their lives adjudicating the evidence put before them. There would be some changes—Hobbs would not be allowed to testify because of a recent Supreme Court ruling stating that undercover testimony was admissible only if the officer did not initiate the conversation. Also, the defence was informed that Michalowsky was too ill to testify.

The Crown was going into the trial with a fully loaded arsenal. Witnesses who hadn't testified at the first trial were being called this time. The plan was to inundate the jury with enough evidence that it would be almost bullied into finding Morin guilty. While the first few days of trial, much like those of the first trial, were devoted to technical witnesses and expertise, the defence quickly began jumping on Crown witnesses during cross-examination.

Pinkofsky vilified Crown witness Constable Robertson, who had assisted in the search for Jessop with his dog Ryder on the night of October 3. Ryder had become agitated around Morin's Honda after sniffing one of Jessop's sweaters, but Robertson did not testify at the first trial. He had never been an actual police dog handler. Furthermore, he testified that the sweater he was given to give Ryder the scent was a blue knitted sweater, similar to the sweater the police had been searching for since Jessop's body was found. He said he had kept the sweater overnight and then returned it to the search team. It was never found.

A woman named Mary Hester was also put on the stand by the Crown. She told the court that she used to work with British Intelligence, but that her role was too secretive to disclose in court. She said she had seen Morin twice on the night Jessop disappeared, once during the search for Jessop and once in the cab of a truck. On both occasions, Morin had been wearing a trench coat. The implication was that he had been out and about that night, not at home.

Constable Cameron caught a bit of a break when he took the stand. Pinkofsky revealed to him during cross-examination that the first cigarette butt had been found at the body site almost 30 minutes before Cameron had arrived to help. This meant that the constable could not have been the person who left the butt behind.

When Pinkofsky cross-examined Shepherd and Fitzpatrick, he took them through their notebooks, asking why they had referred to Morin as a suspect three days before they first interviewed him. He asked Fitzpatrick why he had made note of the fact that Morin didn't smoke. Fitzpatrick also denied that Nyznyk ever implied that Morin's hair was different from the necklace hair, and he said it was Nyznyk's fault that the hairs from Jessop's classmates had never been examined.

The Crown threw everything it had in its files into the courtroom, hoping something would stick. The three individuals at the Jessop household on the night of Christine's funeral all testified about hearing someone outside scream "God help me!" Smith, the first pathologist who had examined Jessop's remains, took the stand and admitted that he had made a few mistakes. He also testified that Morin's pocketknife could have caused the injuries later found to the body. When Pinkofsky presented Smith with three knives the attorney had randomly purchased at a store, Smith conceded that any of those knives could have done the damage as well.

Pinkofsky presented Shephard with fuel logs taken from Morin's car during the search. Morin had diligently recorded his mileage every time he refuelled his car, and the intimation was that if Morin had stopped somewhere for gas on the day Jessop disappeared, he would have made a record in the log. The log for the evidence showed that the fuel logs for June through October of 1984 were missing, even though Shephard's notes said they were there.

The defence was hamstrung, however, by one of Justice Donnelly's rulings. He decided that the defence could not introduce evidence of other suspects into the trial. It was just one of a series of contentious rulings that hindered the defence. It was obvious to everyone in the courtroom, wrote Kirk Makin, that Donnelly had a visible distaste for Pinkofsky, which might have influenced his rulings.

Janet Jessop's testimony had changed again. She told the court she had also heard the screaming on the night of her daughter's funeral and that she knew it had been Morin's voice. She hadn't told the police, but told the Crown in May 1991. She also told the jury that Morin had not attended Christine's funeral, which the Crown contended was evidence of guilt.

May and Mr. X again took the stand, surprising the jury by telling everyone that they had been told they didn't have to testify, but had chosen to anyway. Their testimony was no more compelling than it had been during the first trial.

Nyznyk's, however, was. She told the jury about how a hair found on one of Jessop's parkas matched one found in the Honda, but that the sample had deteriorated. She also confirmed that approximately 150 to 200 other hair and fibre samples had disappeared from the CFS and couldn't be found.

On April 19, 1992, after calling 89 witnesses, the Crown rested its case. The defence called everyone it could think of, trying to shred the Crown's case. A woman who had seen a man driving through Queensville on the night Jessop disappeared told the jury that it had appeared the man was trying to hold down a young girl. A retired trace evidence expert told the court that the necklace hair should never have been used as evidence after being exposed to the weather for three months. Staff Sergeant Albert Baley of the Ontario Provincial Police, an experienced police dog trainer, testified that the behaviour of Robertson's dog did not mean that Jessop had been anywhere near the Honda.

"The dog cannot tell you that Christine Jessop had been in that car," he said.

In another oddball moment, the defence successfully petitioned Donnelly to have Michalowsky testify as a witness. The judge, however, placed certain conditions on his testimony. Neither the judge nor the lawyers wore their robes during the testimony. Michalowsky's doctor was allowed to sit right next to him to monitor his health as he testified, and Michalowsky was permitted to testify from behind a screen, with his back to the court. The measures, however, didn't stop him from crying all the way through his testimony. When questioned about the cigarette butt, he claimed that his memory was poor.

The content of the trial then went from odd to shocking as Donnelly ruled that the defence could examine Ken Jessop, now in his early 20s. Pinkofsky made the decision to call Ken as a witness after receiving disclosure from the Crown that contained some hair-raising admissions. During his time on the stand, Ken testified that he and a pair of friends had repeatedly engaged in sexual behaviour and intercourse with Jessop when she was younger. He told the court that it went on for five years and that it was mostly his friends' idea. He also had other questions to answer—in January 1992 Ken had set fire to the Jessops' old trailer home. It had also been at his insistence that the Jessops go the body site the day they found Christine's bones. He told the court he had been motivated to do so by of a series of dreams he'd had.

Morin's four days on the stand did not aid his defence. He spoke very softly, making it difficult for the jury to hear him. For reasons no one could guess, Pinkofsky tendered a stack of Morin's receipts from different businesses the young man had visited, which were stamped for times around 5:30 PM, but didn't submit any from October 3. When Morin broke down and started to cry, rather than let him take a break, Pinkofsky started yelling at him.

When Morin left the stand, the defence rested its case. One hundred and thirty witnesses had taken the stand, but there was one more person to hear from—Justice Donnelly. In a charge to the jury that would later be vilified, Donnelly expressed some clear opinions that the jury might have taken as truth. He dismissed the trivial arguments about the cigarette butt, but said that some weight should be given to the testimony of Hester, the woman who claimed to work for British Intelligence. He questioned the testimonies of the defence's forensic experts but lauded the prosecution's. He also put forward a theory that neither side had offered during the trial—that Jessop had been grabbed off the street rather than taken from her home.

It took the jury eight days to wade through nine months of evidence and offer up a verdict. The decision that came was as unexpected as the verdict in the first trial. On July 30, 1992, the jury found Morin guilty of first-degree murder.

Donnelly sentenced Morin to life in prison with no possibility of parole for 25 years. Pinkofsky wasted no time in launching his appeal. The hearing was scheduled for January 23, 1995, but would never come to pass.

During the period leading up to the scheduled hearing, both the Crown and the defence learned that the technology used to test DNA from fluid samples had become more sophisticated and could now be used with smaller samples. The Crown dispatched a sample of Jessop's semen-stained underwear for analysis. The results came back three days before the appeal was to be heard—Morin's DNA did not match that found in Jessop's panties.

Two days later, Morin was released from jail.

~

On June 26, 1996, the Ontario government ordered a Royal Commission to investigate what had gone wrong in Morin's conviction. Judge Fred Kaufman, a former justice of the Quebec Court of Appeal, began hearings on February 10, 1997, and, over the course of 146 days, heard from 121 witnesses and received 10,000 pages of documents as evidence. Kaufman's report spared no one as he lambasted the CFS for shoddy work, the Durham and York Regional Police for the way they conducted the investigation, Michalowsky for his behaviour and the police for the weight with which they had treated informant, fibre and hair evidence. In the end, Kaufman filed 119 recommendations to help prevent a similar failure of justice from happening again.

"We would never know if Guy Paul Morin would ever have been exonerated had DNA results not been available. One can expect that there are other innocent persons, swept up in the criminal process, for whom DNA results are unavailable," Kaufman wrote in his conclusion.

The government of Ontario has since apologized to Morin and paid him a $1.25-million settlement.

To date, the murder of Christine Jessop has not been solved. There are no new suspects.

Chapter Four

Thomas Sophonow

Winnipeg, Manitoba
March 15, 1982

J ohn Doerkson had the worst possible luck. The Winnipeg man had just been standing outside the city courthouse, waiting for the first court appearance of that guy the police had finally arrested for killing Barbara, when it happened.

One minute he was inside the courtroom trying to get a better look at the guy he might have seen outside the dough- nut shop back in December, and the next he was in the back of a police squad car, bound for lock-up at the Winnipeg Public Safety Building.

And why? All because of a lousy unpaid traffic ticket.

Doerkson shook his head as he made his way through the Remand Centre, past other men temporarily jailed for var- ious crimes. How could that cop have possibly known that Doerkson hadn't paid the fine? The cop had just come up to him on the street, asked for his name and then called it in to dispatch. The next thing Doerkson knew, he was being informed that he was under arrest—all for a lousy hundred bucks.

Doerkson shuffled along, following his guards, making his way to his cell for however long it would take to pony up the dough to pay the damned fine, when it happened. He looked up just as a tall, lanky man in glasses and a moustache walked past him going the opposite direction.

Doerkson froze on the spot. He craned his neck as the other man continued walking past. When the man was gone, Doerkson looked down at the newspaper he was carrying. He flipped a few pages but knew even before he got to the right place that he was correct.

The composite drawing stared back at him. The man who had just walked past was a dead ringer for the charcoal sketch. Both appeared to be the same man Doerkson had grappled with back on that fateful night.

He continued walking, remembering again the man in the cowboy hat who had walked out of the Ideal Donut Shop on December 23 and told both him and another man waiting outside that the store was closing early. Doerkson had instantly believed that something was wrong and decided to follow the tall man in the cowboy hat and boots. He had kept the stranger in view while making a brief stop at a Domo gas station to borrow a baseball bat.

He could see it all again: watching as the man started making his way across the Norwood Bridge, seeing the man's hand suddenly spring out from his side and toss something over the bridge's edge. Doerkson remembered dropping the bat, confronting the man and then backing off in fear as the cowboy pulled a knife and used it to drive Doerkson away.

I need to see him again, Doerkson thought to himself, and grabbed the attention of one of the guards.

"Can you show me where Thomas Sophonow is?" he asked.

"I guess," the guard shrugged and started walking him over to a wall of cells. They stopped just before one of the cells, and the guard nodded towards the figure inside.

"That's him."

It's him. He was sure it was the same man. Sophonow was the one who had killed Barbara Stoppel three months ago.

"I need a phone," Doerkson demanded. It was time to do something about this.

Within minutes he was explaining his story to the Crown prosecutor in charge of the investigation.

～

He was a strange man, everyone agreed.

Manitoba might be the natural border of the wild, open prairies of neighbouring Saskatchewan and Alberta, but there weren't too many people who actually walked around pretending to be a cowboy. But here was this guy, stubble, glasses, acne and all, parading around the St. Boniface district of Winnipeg in a pair of cowboy boots and a tall cowboy hat. If he was trying to be subtle, he wasn't doing a very good job of it.

It seemed like everyone saw him do something strange on the afternoon and evening of December 23, 1981, yet no one was able to agree on who he actually was. A pair of shoe store employees saw a creepy-looking guy in a cowboy hat and cowboy boots come into their store that afternoon, ask about a pair of cowboy boots and then leave again.

Three employees at a McDonald's across the street from the Ideal Donut Shop saw a man in western regalia in their restaurant. It had been his second visit in the last week. During the first, he'd been chatty. This time he just sat there, sipping coffee, staring out the window and across the street.

Lorraine Janower was getting antsy because her store, a pharmacy, closed soon and she wanted to get going. She decided, however, to take one last coffee break at around 8:00 PM. Just as she crossed the street, a tall man in a cowboy hat walked into the Ideal Donut Shop, turned around, locked the doors and walked to the back of the restaurant. Janower tried the doors, but they were definitely locked. She walked back to the pharmacy and noticed that her husband, Norman, was sitting in the car outside, waiting to drive her home.

"Keep an eye on the doughnut shop," she said to him as she went back into her store. "There might be something weird going on."

Back inside the pharmacy, Janower looked up again and saw the same tall man unlock the restaurant doors, turn the OPEN sign to the side that read CLOSED and then hustle away.

Myron Zuk, who ran a TV repair shop located nearby, saw the man come from the back section of the restaurant, but he also saw the cowboy make a stop at the restaurant's till and take something from it before unlocking the door, turning the sign around and hustling off.

Mildred King had just parked her car in a nearby parking lot and was making her way towards a friend waiting nearby when she lost her balance. As she fell, she was almost bowled over by a tall man in a cowboy hat walking quickly away from the doughnut shop. King looked around, but didn't see anyone else.

It all seemed too strange to Norman Janower, who also saw the man switch the sign and leave. Knowing his wife still had a few minutes until she was off work, he left his car and walked over to the doughnut shop. He tried the door and found that it was now unlocked, even though the sign said CLOSED. He took a deep breath and dashed inside, looking around. Except that no one was in the establishment, there seemed to be nothing wrong inside the restaurant.

Janower made his way to the back of the restaurant, remembering that the man in the cowboy hat had emerged from there. He found the washrooms and gingerly opened the door to the ladies' room. He poked his head around and gasped, and then turned and bolted.

"Someone call the police," he shouted. It was shortly after 8:30.

~

By all accounts, the police and an ambulance arrived between 8:43 and 8:45 PM. The scene that awaited them was urgent and slightly gruesome.

Barbara Stoppel, 16, was lying on the ground, barely breathing. The young high school student who worked at Ideal to make a little extra spending money was sprawled on the floor of the bathroom. Her lip was bloody and her face was bruised. The most shocking part of the crime scene, however, was the length of twine tied tightly around her neck. There were no signs of sexual assault. The police found $24, likely her bimonthly pay from her work at the doughnut shop, inside her purse.

When the paramedics arrived on scene, they found Stoppel unresponsive. They quickly removed the twine, which was bagged and tagged by the police, and then scooped Stoppel onto a gurney and took off for the nearest hospital, St. Boniface. By the time the doctors got to her, she was already in a coma.

She was hooked up to life support equipment while the hospital tried to find her parents.

When the police started investigating, their prospects for finding Stoppel's assailant looked good. Several people had congregated outside the doughnut shop and told the police about the man they'd seen inside the restaurant before Stoppel's body had been found. They all agreed that he was tall, wore glasses and had a bushy moustache. He had a rash or pimples or some kind of acne on his face, and he looked unkempt, with stubble on his chin. More importantly, he had been wearing a cowboy hat and a pair of cowboy boots.

Police officers fanned out through the nearby parking lot, running licence plates and checking for any out-of-province tags. None were found.

~

The on-duty constable at St. Boniface hospital took the phone from the nurse's outstretched hand and cradled it between his ear and shoulder. It had been a busy morning. Police officers, doctors, nurses and family members had been in and out of the hospital since the Stoppel girl had arrived. The prognosis, everyone knew, was grim.

The voice on the other end of the phone was a little slurred—the officer could tell that the man had obviously spent the preceding few hours drinking. But the officer quickly decided that this was no ordinary drunk. His story might be the most important of all those the police had heard so far.

The man's name was John Doerkson, and he'd been standing outside the doughnut shop when a man in cowboy boots and a cowboy hat had left and told those waiting outside, "We're closing early." According to his statement, Doerkson had become suspicious and decided to follow the man, borrowing a baseball bat from a nearby gas station. When the pair had reached the Norwood bridge, Doerksen said, he saw the man throw something over the side. At that moment, having decided that even though he was substantially shorter than the cowboy, he could handle him, Doerkson had tried to stop him. The man had waved a knife at Doerkson, warning him to back off.

What the police found strange was Doerkson's behaviour after the confrontation on the bridge. He acknowledged that he had returned to the doughnut shop to find a gaggle of police officers, paramedics and rubberneckers milling around. He'd asked around and found out that the girl inside, whom Doerkson knew, had been beaten up. But he hadn't reported to the nearest police officer what he'd seen and done. Instead, he'd hailed a taxi and gone looking for the suspect. When he decided that he wasn't going to be able to locate the man, Doerksen had gone home and started drinking. A few hours later he'd called St. Boniface hospital to see how Stoppel was doing.

Based on Doerkson's statements, the police went to the Norwood Bridge to take a look around. They didn't find any signs of a struggle on the bridge, but they did find something resting on the ice of the Red River, which ran below it. Officers retrieved a box from the ice that contained two items—a pair of gloves and a length of twine.

Two days later, a man no one recognized made a surprise appearance at the hospital to visit Stoppel. Terry Arnold told Barbara's mother that he was a long-distance trucker who often stopped in at the Ideal Donut Shop, that he knew Barbara quite well and that he wanted to see how she was doing. The police, following procedure, took Arnold aside and asked him a few questions. He admitted that he knew Stoppel very well, but provided an alibi to the police that was later verified: he'd been in a restaurant at the time the attack took place. A waitress at the restaurant confirmed that Arnold's story was true.

The police quickly got the different eyewitnesses together with a sketch artist to develop a composite drawing of the cowboy everyone claimed to have seen. The sketch was immediately released to the media and was featured in newspapers and television news broadcasts. Tipsters started phoning in, saying the sketch resembled a number of different people. But one name stood out. An anonymous person called in and said the sketch closely resembled his friend Terry Arnold.

Arnold did bear some resemblance to the man the eyewitnesses had seen, right down to the acne some had remembered. He also lived three blocks away from the doughnut shop—he could see the restaurant from his apartment. Again the police brought Arnold in, and the trucker repeated his story, even admitting he had a little crush on the young waitress. But with his alibi firm, the Winnipeg City Police took no further action to try to place Arnold at the scene.

Five days after arriving at the hospital, Stoppel died, never having recovered from the coma. The police officially upgraded their investigation from one of aggravated assault to murder.

∽

It took Detective Sergeant Bill Van Der Graff a long time to place the face in the composite sketch.

The police had no suspects for Stoppel's murder. Unaccustomed to violent crime, especially murder, the people of Winnipeg were starting to get nervous. So were the mayor and the chief of police. Everyone wanted the killer found, but it seemed that with so much time having elapsed since the murder, the people just wanted the police to capture a suspect, period.

It was now late January. Van Der Graff searched and eventually found the name of the man he was looking for. The previous summer, he had taken a statement from a Vancouver man who admitted to giving a hitchhiker a ride to Winnipeg. The woman had subsequently disappeared and was never found.

Van Der Graff fingered the name on the file: Thomas Sophonow. The more he read through the file, the more warning bells started to sound in his head. He put the file down, picked up the phone and dialed the number for the Vancouver Police Department.

~

A person's history can make him or her a suspect, and Sophonow had history.

Born in Vancouver in 1953, he had dropped out of school in Grade 12. He had spent some of his younger days in prison for committing property crimes, but he seemed to have turned a corner in life. He worked as a doorman at a night club and had even taken the steps to secure a pardon so he could become a Big Brother.

Any suspect with a criminal record, even if it's a youth record, will climb to the top of an investigator's list because of the prevailing belief within the law enforcement community that past behaviour is the best predictor of future behaviour. While Sophonow's record had nothing to do with murder, having a record at all made him attractive to Van Der Graff and the rest of the Winnipeg City Police. Coupled with the fact he was the only suspect of note at the moment, Sophonow seemed as likely a candidate as anyone else to have killed Stoppel.

On a request from the Vancouver Police Department, Sophonow attended a brief interview at police headquarters on March 3. He was open with the detectives, explaining that he had indeed been in Winnipeg on the day in question. He explained that he'd arrived from Vancouver the day prior in the hopes of visiting his estranged wife and two children. He hadn't been able to find them, though. After making a stop at his in-laws' Winnipeg home, he had talked to his wife, Nadine, on a payphone for a few minutes. He'd stopped somewhere for coffee and then left town.

While the interview seemed casual, it would later become one of the most contentious parts of the Crown's case against Sophonow. According to the Vancouver detective's notes, Thomas Sophonow had stated that he "could have been in Ideal Donut Shop, 49 Goulet." But he hadn't been given the chance to look over the officer's notes or sign off on a statement. The detective hadn't offered him the opportunity because he was afraid Sophonow would destroy the notes. Sophonow would later contend that he had actually said he "could not have been in Ideal Donut Shop, 49 Goulet."

The Vancouver detective left the interview with the impression that Sophonow had been genuine and honest with him. He advised the Winnipeg City Police of the interview and its results and then forgot the matter entirely.

The Winnipeg detectives, however, were not satisfied. Nine days later, a pair of police officers hopped on a plane bound for Vancouver. After picking Sophonow up in a local police car, they drove him to the Vancouver Public Safety Building for another interview.

This interview lasted five hours and, compared to the first, was far from a cordial exchange of ideas and stories. The pair of

Winnipeg officers "forgot" to caution Sophonow and advise him of his right to speak to an attorney. Instead they told him they had witnesses who had told the police they had seen Sophonow walking out of the Ideal Donut Shop on December 23 and that he'd been wearing a cowboy hat. Sophonow denied everything, but did confess to owning a cowboy hat, which he claimed he never wore in public.

Sophonow, however, was revealing little else that might help account for the time he spent in Winnipeg that day. Again, what the officers wrote in their notes from that day differed markedly from what Sophonow claimed he had actually said. He was not permitted to review the notes, and the pair of detectives decided they finally had enough evidence to make an arrest. On March 12, Sophonow was charged with the second-degree murder of Barbara Stoppel. For reasons no one has been able to explain, the officers strip-searched Sophonow, inspected his anal cavity for drugs or contraband and then locked him up in a cell.

~

Sophonow was not alone lodged in his cell at the Vancouver Public Safety Building. He had a roommate, Constable Trevor Black, who was there to try to elicit a confession from Sophonow while posing as his cellmate. Sophonow never confessed, although he did make a comment that he was looking forward to getting a free trip back to Winnipeg.

He was quickly transported back to Winnipeg. His bail denied, Thomas Sophonow was left to languish at the Winnipeg

Remand Centre while the police continued to bolster their case against him. One by one, the witnesses who had seen the man now dubbed the "cowboy killer" were brought into the police station and asked to view either a photo lineup or live lineup of potential suspects.

None of the witnesses fared particularly well during the lineups. The photo lineup was eventually discarded because of all the photos on the card, Sophonow's was the only one taken outside. It was also larger than the other photos, which made his picture more prominent. When it came to viewing Sophonow in a lineup room surrounded by other men with similar features, none of the witnesses were able to state with certainty that Sophonow was the man they had seen at the doughnut shop. Doerksen, the man who had followed the killer with a baseball bat and then tried to restrain him, couldn't even pick Sophonow out of the lineup. The other witnesses—Mildred King and Lorraine and Norman Janower—all indicated that Sophonow seemed similar to the cowboy killer, but attributed the similarity to either his height, his weight or the way he walked.

While leaving the police station, Norman Janower asked one of the detectives if he had "picked the right guy." The officer responded that Janower had, in fact, selected the suspect the police were investigating.

As the time drew near for Sophonow's May 17 preliminary inquiry, the case against him was still uncertain. All the police really had were some eyewitnesses who couldn't remember exactly who they'd seen at the crime scene, a witness who claimed the twine found around Stoppel's neck closely matched twine seen in the back of Sophonow's car and Sophonow's lack of an alibi. Some believed it was unlikely that the judge would find enough evidence during the hearing to order Sophonow to stand trial.

And then Doerkson called and everything changed. Mere minutes before Sophonow's hearing was scheduled to commence, an officer performing a spot check on Doerkson outside the courthouse discovered that the man had an outstanding fine for an unpaid traffic ticket. He arrested Doerkson and took him to the cells, where the Christmas tree salesman ran into Sophonow. Doerkson phoned up investigators and explained that he was now certain Sophonow was the man he had chased down the Norwood Bridge on December 23.

The information came just in time to bolster the Crown's case at the preliminary inquiry. It was at this hearing that Sophonow, under the direction of his lawyer, Rocky Pollock, would finally tell the world exactly what he'd been doing when Stoppel had been murdered.

To date, Sophonow had kept quiet about his alibi, stating he felt that how he'd spent his time that evening wasn't "any of their business." But a procession of Crown witnesses, including Doerkson, took to the stand and identified Sophonow as the man they had seen coming out of the coffee shop. The police officers testified about their interviews with Sophonow, mentioning the misleading statements recorded in their note-books that he might have stopped at the Ideal Donut Shop when he was in town.

The accused seldom testifies at his or her preliminary inquiry, and the defence team asks few questions so as not to give the Crown any clues about their defence. But Pollock believed so much in Sophonow's alibi that he decided to put Sophonow on the stand in an attempt to have the judge throw the charges out altogether.

Under Pollock's questioning, Sophonow told the court where he had been and what he had been doing on the night of December 23, 1981. He said he had arrived early in the morning on the day in question, but couldn't find his wife or children. After a visit to his in-laws and a brief call to his wife from a pay phone, Sophonow had spent some time trying to find a former girlfriend of his. When that proved unsuccessful, he had hopped into his car and headed south, bound for the sunny, sandy beaches of Mexico.

About 10 minutes out of Winnipeg, Sophonow had noticed that his car was misbehaving and making strange sounds. He had turned around and eventually found a Canadian Tire, where he asked the mechanic to take a look at his car. This, Sophonow estimated, had occurred at approximately 7:00 PM. While the mechanic was examining the vehicle, Sophonow had gone over to a nearby Safeway, where he purchased approximately 45 prepackaged Christmas stockings for 99 cents each.

He also bought a sandwich, which he took back to the repair shop and shared with a little girl who was waiting with her mother.

The mechanic had stated that Sophonow's car was in need of repair, but that he didn't have the parts to finish the job. The car could probably make it back to Vancouver as long as Sophonow took it easy. After he had paid the bill, Sophonow used a pay phone in the lobby to place a collect call to his mother, telling her he was coming home. According to records tendered by the defence at the preliminary inquiry, the call lasted four minutes, from 7:52 to 7:56.

After leaving the Canadian Tire, Sophonow had driven back into the city and stopped at the Victoria Hospital with the intention of distributing the 45 Christmas stockings to children who were spending the holiday in the hospital. Victoria, however, didn't have a children's ward. The ward clerk on duty that night, Joan Barrett, had told Sophonow of three other hospitals he could try and described where they were and how he could get into them after hours. He had then visited two of the hospitals, dropping off the stockings at the children's wards and then gotten back into his car and started the long trip back east to Vancouver.

Crown prosecutor Wayne Myshkowsky argued that the entire alibi was fabricated, especially because Sophonow hadn't mentioned to the police any of the events that took place after Sophonow had left his in-laws' place. Myshkowsky told Judge

Charles Rubin that the eyewitness evidence alone was enough to warrant committing Sophonow to trial. Rubin agreed and ordered Sophonow to stand trial on one count of second-degree murder in Stoppel's death. Sophonow had already been denied bail—he would await trial behind bars.

～

The trial began on October 18, 1982, when a jury of 10 men and two women was selected. The Crown's case was straightforward. Ignoring the fact that $24 had been found in Stoppel's purse after she was attacked, Crown prosecutor George Dangerfield argued that the motive had likely been one of robbery. He had in his pocket no less than four witnesses who could identify Sophonow as the man in the cowboy hat they had seen at the Ideal Donut Shop on December 23, 1981. Remarkably, every witness who took the stand in the trial did point to Sophonow as the man they had seen, which was strange considering that none of them had been able to positively identify him in a lineup shortly after his arrest.

Dangerfield knew from the preliminary inquiry exactly where Pollock would go with his defence: Pollock would argue that given Sophonow's alibi, he could not have had the time to drive back into town from the Canadian Tire, which he had left around 8:00 PM, kill Stoppel sometime before 8:30 and escape. To counter that argument, a pair of detectives timed a drive from the Canadian Tire to the doughnut shop and found it took them 14 minutes. Although the timeline was tight, Dangerfield believed that Sophonow could have made the trip in time to kill Stoppel.

The police had little to offer in the way of forensic evidence. They were unable to match any hairs, fluids or fingerprints found at the scene to Sophonow. The police had searched every vehicle in the parking lot nearby shortly after Stoppel was found but hadn't found any cars sporting British Columbia licence plates. Stoppel had been dead when she arrived at the hospital, but was kept clinically alive on life support. An autopsy ruled the cause of death as strangulation, but there were other signs of violence as well. Her lips were swollen, there were blood stains on her teeth, as well as on the floor and walls, and a large quantity of saliva had been found inside her sweater. There were no signs the young woman had been sexually assaulted.

On November 2, 1982, Sophonow took the stand in his own defence.

"Did you strangle Barbara Stoppel?" Pollock asked.

"No," Sophonow replied forcefully.

Sophonow spent the next four and a half hours on the stand, retelling the details of his alibi and answering other questions. He explained to the jury that he did own a cowboy hat, but said: "I've never worn it in Winnipeg. It looks ridiculous in public. I've worn it to parties; that's the only times." He denied owning a pair of cowboy boots.

At one point, Dangerfield passed him a copy of the composite sketch of the killer and asked Sophonow if he looked like the killer. Sophonow shot back, "I'll leave that up to the jury to decide."

After 16 days, both the Crown and defence had rested their cases. Pollock was arguing that his client simply hadn't had enough time to make the trip to the doughnut shop and strangle Stoppel, while Dangerfield was trying to get the men and women of the jury to believe that Sophonow had the time.

No one had any idea what the jury was thinking when they left the courtroom to begin deliberations. But as hours passed by without any word from the foreman, the prosecution grew wary and the defence optimistic. Finally, after 28 hours, court reconvened. The foreman rose and announced to the judge that he and the other 11 jurors were deadlocked and could not reach a verdict.

Justice Louis Deniset accepted the foreman's words and declared a mistrial. It was a win for Sophonow in the sense that he had not been found guilty, but he also had not been exonerated. Aware of this, and with the Crown already saying it intended to move for a second trial, Deniset ordered that Sophonow remain behind bars. The second trial was scheduled for February 21, 1983. When Sophonow appeared on that day, he did so in the company of a new lawyer.

Not much had changed in the three months separating Sophonow's trials except for the face of the judge and the defence counsel.

Justice John Scolin presided over the trial, with Dangerfield again leading the prosecution. Sophonow, however, had chosen Greg Brodsky, a tenacious litigator who believed very much in his client's innocence, as his new counsel.

The first few days of the second trial closely mirrored those of the first as a jury was selected and the police took the stand to describe their initial investigation, findings and interviews. It wasn't until Dangerfield began to call eyewitnesses that Brodsky realized he might be in trouble.

Almost every single person who claimed they had seen the cowboy killer had changed their testimony since the first trial to allow Sophonow enough time to make the trip from the Canadian Tire to the Ideal Donut Shop. Lorraine Janower now testified that she had gone to the restaurant closer to 8:15 PM to get a coffee, when she found the door closed. Her husband, Norman, supported the idea.

Dangerfield also dipped into the murky waters of the correctional system to provide even more damning evidence against Sophonow. He called Thomas Cheng, who was in custody on a number of fraud-related charges, to the stand. Cheng told the jury that he and Sophonow had spent time at the Winnipeg Remand Centre together. He claimed that during a game of shuffleboard, Sophonow had confessed that he had killed

Stoppel. Strangely enough, all 28 charges against Cheng were dropped, and, rather than being deported, he was allowed to leave Canada voluntarily six months after the trial ended.

Dangerfield also trotted out Constable Black, the undercover police officer who had shared a cell with Sophonow shortly after his arrest the previous March. Black had not been called as a witness in the first trial, but testified in the second that while in jail, Sophonow had said he had been in the doughnut shop and that he had locked the door from the inside, talked to the waitress and left.

Then there was the issue of the gloves and twine. The gloves alone would generate most of the drama during the second trial. During a cross-examination, Brodsky turned to his client and asked him to put the gloves on. In a scene that would later be repeated in the world-renowned O.J. Simpson trial, Sophonow turned to the jury to show them the results. The gloves didn't fit.

It wasn't enough to convince the Crown that their case was poorly planned and ultimately false. Even the testimony of Joan Barrett, who remembered a man similar to Sophonow coming in on the night of December 23 with an armload of prepackaged stockings, couldn't persuade Dangerfield that he was wrong.

Scolin obviously felt the same way. During his charge to the jury, the judge told them that they should give the same weight to Cheng's testimony as they would give to Barrett's. He even ridiculed Barrett in front of the jury. During her testimony, Barrett had responded that she was "dead sure" that someone had come into the hospital that night with an armload of stockings. Scolin repeatedly referred to Barrett as "the dead sure lady."

With the evidence weighed in the Crown's favour, it came as no surprise that the jury returned relatively quickly. On March 17, almost two years after his arrest, the jury found Sophonow guilty of second-degree murder, and he was sentenced to 20 years in prison.

"I didn't kill her. I thought all you had to do was tell the truth but I was wrong," Sophonow lamented after the verdict.

Brodsky wasted no time launching an appeal of the verdict. He had found Scolin's charge and conduct during the trial to be so prejudicial that most of the appeal was centered around mistakes or questionable comments the trial judge had made. Although it took almost a year, the Manitoba Court of Appeal's three-judge panel agreed to hear the argument. In a two-to-one decision, the majority overturned the conviction and ordered a new trial for Sophonow, his third. The justices found that crucial time elements of the alibi had not been related to some of the Crown witnesses, that the jury should have been warned about believing Cheng's testimony and that Scolin had denigrated Barrett. They also believed that Doerkson was an unreliable witness and that his testimony should no longer be considered.

But Doerkson was on the witness list when the third trial convened on February 4, 1985. The intervening months, however, had brought some interesting revelations, particularly for the defence. Brodsky had received a letter from a former police officer who was serving time for murder stating that members of the police squad investigating Stoppel's death were making the rounds at different jails, offering reduced sentences or favourable parole reports for testimony against Sophonow. When asked if he would testify, the police officer refused.

Another individual came forward with important information but also stated that he wasn't willing to tell his story to the courts. Fermin Wendles was a taxi driver in Winnipeg who had repeatedly given Stoppel rides to and from work. Wendles stated he had thought this was strange because Stoppel lived only a few minutes by foot from the restaurant. When his curiosity got the better of him, Wendles had asked why she was using a taxi when she didn't need to. Stoppel had responded that she was scared because she was receiving threatening phone calls.

Three days later, the police arrested him for an unpaid ticket. According to Wendles, they interrogated him ruthlessly and continually asked him why he would lie for Sophonow. The experience scared Wendles away from the idea of testifying in any capacity.

The third trial walked a fine line between courtroom drama and the purely bizarre. Again the beginning of the trial closely mirrored the first two as the police testified and set the scene for the new jury. But then the Crown started presenting some new elements in its case.

One element that wasn't new was Cheng's testimony; what was new was that he wasn't there to give it. Cheng had since left for Hong Kong, and the Crown, now led by prosecutor Stuart Whitley, asked Justice Benjamin Hewak if the Crown could read Cheng's prior testimony into evidence, even though Cheng himself wasn't available for cross-examination. Despite Brodsky's objections, Hewak let Whitley do just that.

This time around, the Crown pulled no punches in trying to convict Sophonow. Whitley put two well-known convicts on the stand to testify that they had heard Sophonow admit to killing Stoppel.

Adrian McQuade had spent a great deal of his adult life in jail for various property crimes, including theft and breaking and entering. He'd first come to the attention of the police in 1982, when he informed officers that Sophonow had admitted to killing Stoppel. McQuade had said he would be willing to testify in exchange for $10,000. At the time, the police told McQuade exactly what he could do with his testimony. But Whitley had since resurrected the plan, with one exception— there would be no money. McQuade agreed to testify anyway.

After McQuade, Douglas Martin, a confessed heroin addict who claimed he had since cleaned up his act, took the stand. He told the jury he had been serving time at the Prince

Albert Penitentiary in Saskatchewan at the same time as Sophonow and that Sophonow had confessed to him.

There were other twists and turns in the prosecution's case. Whitley was now working from the theory that the attack had been sexual in nature and not a robbery at all. The only evidence he had to corroborate this idea was the large amount of saliva found on Stoppel's body. He called to the stand Colin Dawes, a professor of dentistry, who testified that people who are forced to perform fellatio often salivate excessively. Dawes conceded to Brodsky, however, that chewing gum can also cause people to salivate. A piece of chewing gum had been found on the ground in the washroom and was sent for testing only after Dawes' testimony. The tests indicated that Stoppel had been the one chewing the gum.

Despite the Court of Appeal's strong warning against relying on Doerkson, the Crown called him back to the stand to testify. Norman Janower also took the stand and now testified that he hadn't gone into the doughnut shop to check on Stoppel until closer to 8:40 PM. This allowed ample time for Sophonow to get from the Canadian Tire to the doughnut shop. But it also meant that he would have had much less time to escape, given that the police arrived on the scene at approximately 8:43.

From that point on, the trial descended into the absurd. Though it had been established in the second trial that the gloves found on the frozen Red River did not fit Sophonow, Whitley argued that they didn't have to. Sophonow just had to have worn them at the time of the killing. Furthermore, Whitley declared before the jury, if the gloves fit on his own hands, they must surely fit Sophonow's because he and Sophonow were of similar height and build.

Brodsky objected vehemently, but Hewak allowed Whitley to demonstrate his theory.

"Why wouldn't it be of some relevance to know how a glove fits Mr. Whitley's hand compared to how it fits Mr. Sophonow's hand?" Hewak argued. Whitley put the gloves on. They fit.

When the time came to present his defence, Brodsky came forward with several new witnesses. He put on the stand McDonald's employee Alan Shapiro, who had been working in the restaurant across from the doughnut shop on December 23, 1981. Shapiro testified that a man dressed as a cowboy had been sitting at one of the tables in McDonald's that night around 7:00 PM, sipping coffee and staring out the window. Shapiro also testified that he had seen the man in his restaurant the week before. The testimony was potent—Shapiro had introduced a cowboy who had been in his restaurant at a time when Sophonow was still in Vancouver.

Shapiro examined the composite sketch, and Brodsky asked if it resembled the man Shapiro had seen in his restaurant. Shapiro admitted that it bore a close resemblance. He was then asked whether Sophonow resembled the composite sketch.

"He doesn't," Shapiro stated emphatically.

The McDonald's employee was one of only a handful of defence witnesses. Brodsky had informed the court earlier on that his client would testify only if he was allowed to do so under the influence of sodium amytal, colloquially known as truth serum. A ruling in favour of the practice would have been precedent setting, but Hewak was not in the mood to make legal history. He denied the request, and Sophonow did not testify.

Brodsky ran into another speed bump in presenting his case. Although Joan Barrett was permitted to testify, several other nurses who had seen a man drop off some stockings on the night of the murder were not permitted to tell their stories in court.

When Brodsky finished calling witnesses, both sides made their final arguments, and the case was put to the jury. One day passed without word from the 12 jurors. Then a second, a third and a fourth, all without so much as a question on the evidence from the jury. At one point, the jury sent out a note saying they had reached a verdict. But in the time it took to locate Judge Hewak, another note was dispatched saying they were still deliberating.

After 52 hours of debate, the longest jury deliberation in Canadian history, the court received a note from the jury foreman complaining about one of the jurors, Frances Kuntz. According to the foreman, Kuntz was claiming that she had psychic powers and special gifts. The court reconvened minus the jury, and the Crown argued to have Kuntz removed as a juror. Hewak questioned both the foreman and Kuntz, who claimed she had never said she was psychic, just that she had a "gift for thinking." Over the defence's objections, Kuntz was discharged from her duties as a juror. Within minutes, the remaining 11 jurors entered the courtroom with their verdict— Sophonow was guilty. Kuntz had obviously been the only hold-out in the room.

Brodsky made no secret of the fact that he was planning to appeal the verdict, and he did so as quickly as possible. His arguments turned out to be so persuasive that, on December 12, 1985, the Court of Appeal unanimously ruled that Sophonow should be set free, even before presenting their reasons for the decision. Sophonow was released, and the court's reasons were published three months later. The justices all found that the jury had been instructed poorly, that the evidence had been weak, that Cheng's evidence should not have been read into the record, that Whitley should not have been permitted to try on the gloves found near the crime scene and that the nurses who had seen Sophonow on the night in question should have been allowed to testify.

In overturning the conviction, the justices also shocked the legal community with their final decision: Sophonow, they declared, should not face a fourth a trial. His freedom was now assured.

"I am concerned that it would be difficult, in view of the notoriety the case had gained, to which I made reference…to find a jury of 12 citizens totally uninfluenced by what they had seen or heard already," wrote Justice J.A. Twaddle.

In April 1986, the Supreme Court of Canada refused to hear a counter-appeal by the Manitoba Attorney General seeking to overturn the court's ruling. It slammed the door closed on any further criminal proceedings against Sophonow.

But though the decision was a victory, it was not an exoneration. The court hadn't actually said that Sophonow wasn't guilty of the crime, and the government focused in on this detail. In June of the following year, the NDP government of Manitoba passed legislation stating that only persons who have been found not guilty by a jury could be eligible for compensation or a public inquiry. Because Sophonow had never been acquitted of the charge, he would have to prove his own innocence before any a request for compensation or an inquiry could be entertained.

That didn't stop Sophonow from trying. Broke, unemployed and ostracized by most of the people who knew him, Sophonow launched a lawsuit against the chief of the Winnipeg Police in April 1987. He also repeatedly called on the government to release the gloves in their care for forensic testing. That testing, however, wouldn't occur for another 13 years.

When the truth starts to come out, almost nothing can stop it.

In 1998, the City of Winnipeg announced that it was forming a new task force to investigate the Barbara Stoppel murder. In the course of the investigation, the police took samples of DNA from Sophonow to compare with specimens that had been found at the crime scene.

The samples proved what Sophonow had been saying since his initial arrest in 1981—he was an innocent man.

On June 8, 2000, the Winnipeg City Police issued a formal apology to Sophonow. The government of the day acknowledged Sophonow's innocence and finally took the action he had been waiting for since he had been freed from jail. It issued an apology and ordered a public inquiry to determine both how much compensation Sophonow deserved and how to ensure that a similar situation would never happen again.

As the public inquiry began, the police announced they had a new suspect in their investigation. They were looking long and hard at Terry Arnold, the former long-haul truck driver from Winnipeg who had visited Stoppel at the hospital and had been interviewed shortly afterwards. During their investigation, the police discovered that the woman who had provided Arnold's alibi had, in fact, been lying at his request. She said he had come into the restaurant, shaking and nervous, and asked her to tell anyone who asked that he had been there the whole time. Furthermore, in 1981, Arnold had a bad case of acne and frequently wore a cowboy hat and cowboy boots. At least one person had called the police back in 1982, saying that Arnold was a dead ringer for the suspect in the composite sketch.

Arnold's criminal behaviour since 1981 was also cause for concern. He had been convicted of raping four children in Newfoundland and was sentenced to eight years. In 1997, he was convicted of murdering Christine Browne, who had been found raped and murdered in Keremeos, BC, in 1991. He was released in 2002 on appeal, and the Crown eventually stayed the charge against him. Police forces across the country, including in Winnipeg, were investigating him in as many as three other murders. In 2001, the Winnipeg police obtained a warrant for one of Arnold's palm prints.

Unfortunately, there would be no closure for the Stoppel family. In March 2005, the police found Arnold's body inside his Victoria home. He had committed suicide by overdosing on drugs and had left behind a note stating he was not responsible for killing anyone.

The public inquiry into the wrongful convictions of Sophonow wrapped up after eight months of hearings and testimony from 63 witnesses. In the end, Justice Peter Cory suggested that Sophonow be compensated by the City of Winnipeg, the Province of Manitoba and the federal government for a total of $2.6 million. All three parties immediately accepted Cory's findings, as well as the 43 recommendations he made to ensure no one would suffer a similar ordeal again.

"To tell you the truth, no compensation would pay for all the years," Sophonow later said.

In June 2007, the government also announced the appointment of a former Ontario judge to investigate the behaviour of former Manitoba Crown prosecutor George Dangerfield, who was responsible not only for Sophonow's case, but also for James Driskell's, another man convicted for a murder he did not commit. To date, 12 inmates who were prosecuted by Dangerfield are claiming they were wrongfully convicted.

Sophonow now lives in New Westminster, BC.

Chapter Five

Wilbert Coffin

Miami, Florida
November 2, 1958

Just a stoic man, with a few mining claims
When Altoona County cracked their whip,
at him was laid the blame
You see, they got their man, but any man could have killed
You see justice does leave holes that the innocent sometimes fill
— *The Wilbert Coffin Story* by Dale Boyle

O fficers with the Miami Police Department were confused and frustrated. They had in their cells a Native man they had picked up for vagrancy, which wasn't uncommon in these parts of Florida. There were homeless people everywhere.

But this guy wasn't even American. From what few details they'd been able to pry out of him, they'd established that he was Canadian. And he was making some fairly startling claims.

No sooner had the man started talking than one of Miami's officers got on the horn to the Québec Provincial Police (QPP). After all, this guy wasn't trying to defect or live in Florida illegally—he was telling anyone who would listen that he had helped kill two American men and their hunting guide up in the Gaspé peninsula a few years earlier.

But then something strange happened. The man, who claimed his name was Francis Thompson, totally changed his story. Although he'd rattled off the names of the murdered hunters and even correctly answered a series of questions the QPP had requested that the Miami police ask him, Thompson now clammed up entirely. He insisted that he had been lying so he could be transferred back to Canada, where the prisons were in much better shape. He even submitted to a lie detector test about his involvement in the killings. The results came back negative, meaning the polygraph did not detect any signs that he was lying.

Although he had changed his story, Thompson had confessed to a triple homicide. The QPP weren't interested, though. They told the Miami Police Department that as far as they were concerned, the case of the murdered hunters had been solved years ago. They had arrested a man who had been seen in the company of the hunters and who also had an excellent understanding of the forested lands where the trio had gone bear hunting for three weeks one June. He was a veteran of World War II, a prospector and a jack of all trades who spent quite a bit of time in Gaspé.

His name was Wilbert Coffin. He had been convicted of first-degree murder in the death of one of the members of the hunting party. The motive, the Crown had contended, was robbery because $650 had gone missing from the victim's wallet.

Coffin also happened to be dead. Despite an appeal, a Cabinet-ordered review of the case by the Supreme Court of Canada and a last-ditch plea for clemency, Coffin had been executed at the Bordeaux prison in Quebéc. He had been led to the gallows, kissing his prayer book, asking God over and over again for mercy.

The noose had been positioned around his neck, and the trap door had sprung open, sending Coffin plunging downward. It took him 15 minutes to die.

The scapegoat was dead, but very few people believed he deserved it. In fact, most people believe Coffin hadn't killed anyone.

≈

July 5, 1953

One phone call wasn't enough.

The QPP took the call and listened to a distraught man who said he was calling from Pennsylvania. His son had gone hunting in Québec's Gaspé region with a family friend and his son. They had been due back at the end of June, and it was now the beginning of July. The officer who took the call promised the man that the police would look into the matter. Nothing happened.

It wasn't until the QPP received a second phone call, this one from the Pennsylvania State Police, that they decided to take any action. They took down as much information as they could about the wayward hunters and started putting together a search party.

It wasn't that strange an occurrence for hunters to get lost. American hunters came to the Gaspé all the time in the late spring and early summer months to hunt some of the most prized game in the province, mostly black bear. It was the mainstay of the region's tourism industry and a significant source of provincial revenue. The hunters came to Canada, paid American dollars for local goods and services and went back home with a carcass or two. It was easy money, but valuable all the same.

Eugene Lindsey of Altoona, Pennsylvania, had left his home state for the wilderness of Eastern Canada on June 5 in the company of his 17-year-old son Richard and Richard's friend Frederick Claar, 19. The hunting trip was supposed to last three weeks. By July 5, they hadn't returned home, and no one had heard from them.

It was Claar's father who first contacted the QPP with his concerns about his son. Québec's finest, however, had not bothered acting on his call. Claar instead took his worries to the Pennsylvania state police, who contacted the QPP. Pressed by their comrades to the south, the QPP finally took action and launched a search of the area around the Gaspé Village.

It was difficult to believe that the trio had gotten lost. Lindsey had made frequent trips to the Gaspé to hunt and was known in the community. Yet no one had seen or heard from the party in some time. Police officers and local townsfolk started combing through the woods around the village, looking for some sign that the hunting party had been there recently.

On July 10, they found their first ominous clue. Searchers came across Lindsey's green 1947 pickup truck, apparently abandoned. According to a *Toronto Daily Star* article dated shortly after the search and the testimony of several witnesses years later, the search party also found a crumpled, weathered note under a rock nearby. Dated June 13, the note apparently indicated that the trio had split up and that one of the men, though it was never established whom, had returned to the truck and left the note for the other two to let them know he had been there.

The note mysteriously disappeared. Despite the assertions of several searchers later on, a Royal Commission of Inquiry would state its doubt that the note ever existed. The team also found a second note affixed to the windshield of the truck. It was signed by Clarence Claar, Frederick's father, who was out searching for the trio and left the note for the rest of the search team, indicating that he had already passed the truck.

The searchers fanned out across the wilderness, which was divided into a series of numbered camps. The truck was found approximately one-and-a-half miles from Camp 21. There were few personal belongings left in the truck, but searchers found a rifle in the back.

The first body, when they found it, was in miserable shape. The party had been out hunting bears, and it was obvious that the bears had gotten to the bodies. At first, it was difficult to tell whether or not an animal might be responsible for the man's death because the body was so badly mangled, mauled and decomposed.

But there were clues right from the outset that the death was suspicious in nature. Searchers quickly identified the body as that of Eugene Lindsey—they found his empty wallet nearby. Although the bulk of his remains were found on one side of a nearby stream, a portion of what was later determined to be his scalp was found on the opposite side. The skull fragment was small, but large enough to identify. Neither the search team nor the police ever found Lindsey's head. He had obviously been decapitated.

There were other signs nearby that Lindsey had died at the hands of some*one* rather than some*thing*. A rifle was located near the skull fragment. The stock was damaged—in fact, experts would later state that it appeared the rifle stock had been nicked by a bullet. Embedded in the wood grain of the rifle butt were human hairs, which were later identified as being similar to

Lindsey's. The police quickly began to develop a theory—that whoever had attacked Lindsey had bashed him over the head with his own rifle. Because the head was never located, no one was able to conclusively prove this theory.

It was strange, the police would learn, that Lindsey's wallet was empty. His friends and family testified that the man usually carried large sums of money on his person, often thousands of dollars at a time. Investigators later established that when Lindsey left Altoona, he brought along approximately $650 in American money. All of it was missing.

Some disputed testimony that was revealed years later indicated that searchers found another item, which at the time didn't seem nearly as intriguing as it would later prove to be. Investigators and searchers located at least two empty bottles of American whisky near Lindsey's body. Years later, when several journalists started digging into Lindsey's background, they discovered that he had actually detested the whisky of his homeland. He had an affinity for Canadian whisky and usually brought a bottle or two back home after his hunting trips.

It was not the first odd fact that the public would learn about Lindsey. As reporters, not the police, started asking questions, they found themselves with notebooks full of information that would later cast a pall over the accepted theory of how Lindsey had died.

～

The woods of the Gaspé became increasingly morbid for the search team and continued to offer up strange clues that no one could quite piece together.

The remains of Richard Lindsey and Frederick Claar were located approximately three kilometres from Eugene Lindsey's body. They too had been visibly mauled and disturbed, and it was only Richard's body that would yield any real answers as to how they might have died. Investigators noticed, despite its tattered condition, two bullet holes in his shirt. No bullets were recovered from the body. An examination of Eugene and Frederick's bodies did not reveal how they had died. A search of the area around the bodies did yield another oddity, though— a cigar that witnesses would later say was of the same brand Eugene Lindsey had smoked. They also asserted that neither Richard nor Frederick had ever touched tobacco.

While the search team worked to examine and recover the bodies, they made further baffling finds. As they combed the woods, they kept turning up items that belonged to the ill-fated hunting party, such as sleeping bags and a camp stove. More often than not, these items were found hanging from the branches of trees and shrubs in the area. One of the forensic examiners who responded to the scene, Dr. Jean Marie Roussel, initially stated that it appeared the items had been thrown from a vehicle in motion. There was no other way to explain how some items had ended up so high in the trees. That theory also implied one truth that the investigators and prosecutors later ignored or forgot: it would be difficult for a man driving a vehicle through the bush to throw camping stoves and sleeping bags out of a car or truck as he navigated around trees and brush. There was likely a second person involved.

The police, however, weren't looking for two people. As far as they were concerned, they were looking for only one individual, and they believed they had him already within their grasp.

~

Wilbert Coffin, 42, was one of 11 children born to his parents in Douglastown, Québec. He spent almost his entire life living and working in the Gaspé.

For a man who, like many of his generation, didn't complete a formal education, Coffin had done quite well for himself. He spent five years with the military and served in campaigns in Holland and Italy as a cook during World War II. When he returned, he became a jack-of-all-trades prospector, combing the bush he knew so well for mineral deposits, staking claims and trying to interest companies or investors in them. He was an honest man, devoted to the Anglican Church in a province populated mostly by Catholics and, despite growing up in Québec, spoke hardly a lick of French.

He wasn't married, though that would later become an issue for Coffin. He had been romantically involved with a woman named Marion Petrie, who lived in Montréal, for several years. The pair had a child named James, who was born out of wedlock. Coffin spent his time between Montréal and the Gaspé, either being with his family or plowing through the bush. He kept a camp outside Gaspé where he and his brother Donald sometimes stayed.

When the call went out for searchers to help find the wayward hunting party from Pennsylvania, Coffin had willingly joined in the search. He felt he had to. As he explained to the police, who listened with a curious ear, he was the last person known to have seen Claar and the Lindseys alive.

On June 6, according to Coffin, he had left Montréal in the company of Angus McDonald, a city-dwelling potential investor with little experience out in the bush, to examine several sites that Coffin had staked out in the Gaspé area. Coffin told the police that neither man had a rifle when they had left.

Coffin, it turned out, wasn't allowed to have a rifle. His criminal record was clean, but a park ranger had caught him poaching deer a year earlier. As a result, Coffin was fined and banned from having a firearm while out in the wilderness.

The pair spent some time exploring the area up until June 10. The two were supposed to meet up and head into the bush again on June 10, but Coffin never made the meeting. Convinced that McDonald was slowing him down, Coffin decided to head into the bush on his own.

He told the police that shortly after heading into the wild, he had come across three hunters matching the description of the three Americans who were now dead. They were having problems with their truck and told Coffin they believed the truck's fuel pump had broken down. Always willing to lend a hand, Coffin had driven back into Gaspé with Richard Lindsey to buy a new fuel pump. They successfully tracked one down and headed back out to where the hunters' truck was parked. On the way, Richard had showed off an ornamental hunting knife he had brought along on the trip. After some cajoling by Coffin, Richard had decided to give the knife to Coffin as a thank you for his help. Coffin said he had tried to pay the teen for it, but Richard had refused the offer.

What happened after they had arrived back at the truck has been the source of contention to this day.

According to Coffin, when he and Richard had returned to the site where Eugene Lindsey and Claar were waiting, the pair were no longer alone—two other men had been standing and chatting with the Americans. Coffin said he'd introduced himself to the new arrivals, but could no longer remember their names. He did recall that the pair had claimed they were also Americans.

The vehicle the second hunting party had brought into the bush with them was peculiar and couldn't help but stand out against the green foliage of the Québec wilderness. According to Coffin, the pair had been driving a Jeep that was enclosed in some sort of after-market box. The box had appeared to be made of plywood and was painted yellow. The Jeep, Coffin also recalled, had sported American licence plates.

Eugene Lindsey had then offered Coffin $40 for his time and assistance, which the prospector pocketed along with young Richard's hunting knife. After handing over the fuel pump, Coffin had promised the hunters he would be back in the area in a couple of days and would check in on them then. When he had driven away, the two men were still talking with the Lindsey hunting party.

Coffin, it turned out, was a man of his word. Two days later, on June 12, he returned to the site where he had left the Americans, as he had promised he would. Their truck was still there. He told the police he had waited around for the better part of the day, but saw no sign of either the Lindseys or the two men who had been there with them. While he was waiting, he decided to drink a little bit of liquor to keep himself entertained. Nighttime eventually fell, and there was still no sign of the Lindsey party.

He admitted freely to the police that, under the influence of alcohol, he had acted against his better judgment and helped himself to a few items out of their truck, taking a pair of binoculars, a valise and, strangely, the fuel pump he had helped obtain on June 10.

With no sign of Eugene, Richard or Frederick, Coffin had decided to head back into the Gaspé before returning to Montréal to see his common-law wife and son. It was at this point that the police became interested in him as a suspect.

It wasn't the residents of Gaspé who were crying out for the murders to be solved. It was the American government.

As soon as word reached the press that the bodies of Eugene, Richard and Frederick had been found and that the circumstances were suspicious, the Americans began to grumble publicly. That grumbling was led by a sizeable lobby organization out of the State of Pennsylvania called the Pennsylvania Federation of Sportsmen's Clubs, which at the time boasted approximately 200,000 members. The news that three of their own had been murdered in the Canadian wilderness brought about a swift, loud cry of injustice. Buoyed by the support of Congressman James E. Van Zant, the group began lobbying the State Department of the United States government to pressure the Québec provincial government, headed by Maurice Duplessis, to find the killer and bring him to justice.

Duplessis was well aware of what consequences inaction on the part of the police might bring. American hunters brought their American dollars to the province and spent quite liberally, which the provincial government later snapped up in the form of taxes. If the Federation of Sportsmen's Clubs and the State Department started warning Americans against hunting in Canada, that revenue would dry up quickly. It would cost local people their businesses and jobs.

Depending on who is telling the story, Duplessis is remembered as either a strong leader or the democratic version of a tyrant. He and his Union Nationale party had sailed to government in 1936, led the province until 1939 and then returned to a majority within the National Assembly in 1944. A lifelong bachelor, Duplessis was known as a strong advocate of provincial rights within Confederation, preferring that the provinces look after their own people and problems, with minimal oversight from the federal government of the day.

But Duplessis' government was rife with patronage, and the premier himself was not above using his political powers to suppress opposition to his rule. He passed laws trying to limit the rights of unions, Communists and even Jehovah's Witnesses. He used force to disperse organized labour strikes and constantly berated the federal government for intruding on provincial affairs.

So when the State Department came calling, asking for a quick resolution to the murders of the three American hunters, Duplessis acted quickly. Not wanting to deny his province one of its trademark economic pillars, he called on the QPP to get to work.

In response, the force sent one of its most hard-nosed, aggressive officers down to the Gaspé to oversee the investigation. Captain Alphonse Matte was convinced of Coffin's guilt before any of the evidence even hinted that the prospector might be responsible. It was the combination of political pressure and tunnel vision that would eventually cost Coffin his life.

~

Because he was the last person to have seen the three members of the hunting party alive, Coffin was ordered to be held as a material witness shortly after he joined the search party. His detention, however, was just a ruse while the QPP built a case against him.

The police were particularly interested in Coffin's actions and behaviour after he had emerged from the bush on June 12. According to witnesses in the nearby village, Coffin had gone around town spending money lavishly. He had repaid debts, spent time in the beer parlour and even visited the barber. In more than one transaction, he had handed over large bills in American currency.

That testimony caught Matte's attention. The QPP had already established that Eugene Lindsey was known to carry large sums of money and that when he left Altoona, he had apparently jammed $650 American into his wallet. The money was missing from the wallet found near his remains.

It all crystallized in Matte's mind—it was a robbery. Coffin had somehow lured Richard and Frederick away from Eugene, killed them and then tracked Eugene down and killed him as well, helping himself to the contents of Eugene's wallet. With the money in hand, Coffin had gone on a spending spree, dishing out American cash in Gaspé until he had returned to Montréal.

Matte didn't bother wondering why Coffin had willingly returned to the scene of the crime to volunteer his services or why a guilty man would offer a potentially incriminating story that could not be corroborated by any independent source. He didn't wonder why, if the motive was robbery, Coffin had taken only the valise, binoculars and fuel pump, leaving more expensive items like the rifle inside the hunting party's truck.

Coffin tried to explain to the police that after emerging from the bush, he had visited several people who owed him money, either personally or for his services as a prospector. In the end, he had accumulated $580 on his own, some of which was American. He would later provide a detailed list to the police of exactly whom he had visited and how much they had given him, but there is no evidence that the QPP ever bothered following up on it.

On July 27, 1953, a coroner's inquest was convened to investigate the circumstances of the deaths of Eugene Lindsey, Richard Lindsey and Frederick Claar. The goal of an inquest is to attempt to determine responsibility for a questionable death. There is a rumour, never substantiated, that the jury was originally on the verge of exonerating Coffin for the deaths of the three hunters when prosecutor Noël Dorion asked to speak privately with the group. After Dorion left, the jury returned with a verdict on August 27: Coffin, they announced was criminally responsible for the death of Richard Lindsey.

Coffin was kept in custody as the police continued to build the case they would later bring to trial to try to prove his guilt.

One issue the police were having difficulty explaining was that of the murder weapon.

Although he was charged with first-degree murder, Coffin faced only one count for the death of Richard Lindsey. No one had been able to determine exactly how Eugene Lindsey or Frederick Claar died.

It was obvious that Richard had been shot, but the police were so far unable to determine where the murder weapon was. It didn't appear that he had been killed by one of the hunting party's own rifles because there was no evidence that they had been fired. They also knew that Coffin was not supposed to own a rifle.

But Coffin admitted he did have access to a gun. He said he had borrowed a rifle in June from a friend of his named Jack Eagle, but he claimed he had left it at home and never took it into the bush. One of the police officers involved in the investigation later overheard a conversation between Coffin and his brother Donald in which the two apparently discussed the rifle. While the police didn't know the details of what the two talked about, they knew that Donald had left with tears in his eyes. Based on the little information the police had, a search team descended on the Coffin camp. Despite their best efforts, they never found a rifle or any other firearm. They did, however, find truck tire tracks at the gate leading up to the camp. A witness later testified that, on August 28, the day after the conversation between Coffin and Donald had occurred, he had heard a truck in the area, but hadn't actually seen it. The QPP, and subsequently the Crown, automatically inferred that the truck belonged to Donald, who must have come back to the camp to dispose of the murder weapon.

 ⌐∽

While the police were concentrating all of their efforts on proving Coffin's guilt, his family was pooling all of its resources to find him a capable lawyer.

That seemed to have been taken care of early on. The Coffin family hired Alphonse Garneau, who tried shortly after Coffin's arrest to visit his client in custody. Matte, however, informed Garneau that he would have to obtain permission from the Attorney General of Québec, a post held by Premier Duplessis, to do so. (The Canadian Charter of Rights and Freedoms was, at this point, still almost 30 years away). Instead, Garneau sent a letter to Coffin through Matte advising his client to keep his mouth shut until the two were able to meet.

Matte, however, did not pass the letter on to Coffin. He sent it instead to Duplessis, who didn't bother sending it to its intended recipient. As a result, Coffin spoke openly with the police and gave them much of the information they would later use against him at trial.

Weeks after the Coffins hired Garneau, a man named Raymond Maher tracked down Coffin's father at his home and told the older man that it would be in his son's best interests to fire Garneau and hire Maher instead. Maher was apparently very convincing because Coffin's father did exactly that.

It would prove to be one of the biggest mistakes the family ever made.

~

The preliminary inquiry was not quite the formality it appeared to be. Although in the end, Judge Jos. Duguay ordered Coffin to stand trial for one count of first-degree murder, he also admitted that he had almost dismissed the case entirely.

The Crown's case, after all, was entirely circumstantial. They had no direct evidence, forensic or eyewitness, tying Coffin to the death of Richard Lindsey. They had his own admission that he had spent time with the Lindsey party, his spending habits in the days after he last saw them and hearsay testimony about a gun Coffin had borrowed that no one could find.

The police, however, didn't bother looking into Eugene Lindsey's background. If they had, they might have found out that Lindsey was not the upstanding citizen everyone believed he had been. Although he worked at a local railway manufacturer, he was also a moneylender for some of his co-workers. He cashed their cheques, usually keeping any change as his fee. He was also known to lend out money to those who needed it and demand payment with his fists if the borrower didn't pay him back quickly enough.

The police believed they had their man and were determined to take him to trial. The province even sent in two of its best Crown prosecutors, Paul Miquelon and Noël Dorion, both of whom had experience in capital cases. The trial, which began on July 12, 1954, and would continue until August 5, was so packed with drama from start to finish that every portion of it seemed to warrant an appeal. The tiny community of Percé was selected as the venue for the proceedings. When the time came to select a jury, Maher argued that because his client spoke only English, the jury should be made up entirely of anglophones. Justice Gérard Lacroix ruled against the motion, stating that only half the jury would be filled with English speakers. In the end, 12 men were selected to hear the case.

The Crown had been looking for other witnesses to bolster its case and decided to try using some of Coffin's cellmates as witnesses to a confession. During his pre-trial custody, Coffin was housed at the Québec City jail with two people—Réal Marleau and a man named Morin. Each was approached by Matte and asked to testify that Coffin had confessed to the murder. While Marleau refused to say anything of the sort, Morin decided to take the Crown up on its offer. It didn't seem to strike anyone as odd that Morin spoke only French and Coffin only English.

While being transported from the jail to Percé for the trial, Morin asked for and was granted permission to visit with his mother. During his visit, he told his mother what was going on. Alarmed, she contacted lawyer François Gravel, who was assisting Maher with the defence, and told him that her son had no idea what he was talking about and was being duped by the Crown. When Morin arrived in Percé, he refused to testify and was shipped back to Québec City.

The Crown, however, had found one witness who could help their case. A man named Wilson McGregor testified that he had been speaking with Coffin shortly after the prospector returned from the bush, and McGregor had seen the tip of a rifle in the back of Coffin's truck. No one bothered asking McGregor how he could have seen the barrel of a rifle when he had been standing approximately eight metres away from the truck and it had been nighttime.

Miquelon and Dorion tried to use some questionable forensic evidence to prop up their case against Coffin. They called to the stand Bernard Péclet, a chemist who worked with the provincial lab. He explained to the jury that he had examined Richard's clothing and found that whoever shot the young man had used bullets that did not contain potassium nitrate. Only certain calibres of rifle used bullets that did not contain the compound, including the .32-40 rifle Eagle had lent Coffin. On cross-examination, however, Péclet admitted that just because he hadn't found potassium nitrate on the body didn't mean Eagle's rifle had been used to kill Richard.

"Is it possible that the bullet that caused the perforation contained potassium nitrate, and yet, at the time you made your examination, you were unable to find traces of it?" Maher asked.

"Yes, sir," the chemist replied.

Halfway through the trial, the drama surged again with an accusation by the Crown. Matte stood up in front of the court and informed the judge that they had reason to believe that Maher, in the company of a former employee named Jean-Guy Hamel, had found Eagle's rifle and, instead of turning it in as evidence, had disassembled it and thrown it into the St. Lawrence river from the top of the Québec Bridge. Maher vociferously denied the claim, but construction workers in the area later found a piece of a rifle in the river. Hamel was called to testify by the Crown after confessing to the police, but when he took the stand, he denied having any involvement. In a separate trial, he was found guilty of perjury and sentenced to five years in prison.

With the Crown's case winding down, Maher inexplicably disappeared from Percé for a couple of days. Upon his return, the defence lawyer stated to anyone who would listen, "I made a 1,500-mile trip during which I interviewed more than 50 people. This sudden trip was made in Coffin's interest…. We found 85 witnesses that we previously knew nothing about."

Both the spectators and jury were taken aback by the size of the defence Maher was proposing. Meanwhile, the Crown's case seemed to be proceeding as planned. Police witnesses who were called to the stand answered the questions put to them but were careful not to provide any extra information. In one case, though, Sergeant Henry Doyon was prepared to testify that he had seen tire marks consistent with a Jeep near the crime scene, but he was never asked about it.

Even Coffin's common-law wife, Marion Petrie, was called to the stand as a Crown witness. The move, however, backfired when Petrie told the court that Coffin had told her about the two Americans and the mysterious yellow jeep. Scrambling to keep their case under control, the Crown requested and was allowed to cross-examine Petrie, an action that typically is not permitted in the courts.

When the Crown announced that it had finished tendering its case, all eyes in the courtroom turned to Maher to see which of the scores of defence witnesses he was going to call first. Maher calmly stood, looked up at Justice Lacroix and stated for all to hear, "My Lord, the defence rests."

The courtroom was filled with bewilderment. Days after stating he had travelled far and away in search of witnesses to aid his client's defence, Maher was simply throwing in the towel. Coffin would later reveal that he had wanted desperately to testify, but Maher had talked him out of it.

No one has been able to establish exactly what Maher was thinking at the time. He might have believed that he had done such a good job cross-examining the Crown's witnesses that no defence was necessary. He might have simply been a very bad lawyer. Whatever his reasoning, his decision proved incredibly detrimental to his client.

The jury, it turned out, had been waiting to hear Coffin explain himself. They weren't entirely sold on the Crown's theory of the crime and wanted to hear what the defendant had to say. When that didn't happen, the decision was easy.

"A man who does not defend himself must be guilty," one juror later said.

The decision was swift. After 30 minutes of deliberations, the jury said that Coffin was guilty of the first-degree murder of Richard Lindsey. Under the Criminal Code of Canada, the punishment for such an offence was death.

Wilbert Coffin, now 43, was sentenced to hang.

Over the next two years, Coffin's death sentence was delayed seven times as François Gravel, who had taken over as his attorney, tried to have the verdict overturned. His efforts, however, bore little fruit. The Court of Queen's Bench (Appellate Division) turned down the first appeal, stating that "murder had no doubt been committed…a triple murder with robbery as the motive."

Gravel then petitioned the Supreme Court of Canada to hear the case, but Justice John Abbott, a former finance minister for the federal government, turned down the request without conferring with his peers on the bench.

Condemned to die, with his hopes of reprieve growing increasingly dim, Coffin resorted to drastic action. The jack of all trades took a bar of soap in hand to his prison cell and started whittling. On September 6, 1955, Coffin brandished the soap, now resembling a revolver, threatening a pair of prison guards with it. The guards offered no resistance, handing over their keys. Coffin fled the prison, leaving behind a letter asking the authorities for forgiveness.

Outside the prison, Coffin flagged down a taxi driven by Gaston Labrecque. After telling him to drive, Coffin confessed who he was to the driver, showed him the fake gun and told him what he had used it for.

As a woodsman and prospector, it would have been a simple matter for Coffin to vanish into Québec's wilderness and avoid the hangman's noose. But instead of running, Coffin asked Labrecque to take him to Maher's home—Gravel was out of town. Labrecque waited outside in his taxi as Maher and Coffin conferred inside the lawyer's home. After about 30 minutes of conversation, Coffin returned to the taxi and asked Labrecque to take him back to jail. As Labrecque manoeuvred the taxi through the early morning traffic, Coffin laid down on the floor of the taxi for fear of being shot by an overzealous police officer. Labrecque dropped him off at the prison gates, and Coffin returned to his cell without further incident.

"If I had been a guilty man, I would never have gone back to the Québec jail after my escape," Coffin later said.

His prospects, however, weren't good. Gravel managed to convince the Supreme Court to hold a rare hearing in which the lawyer would ask the justices to overturn Justice Abbott's decision not to hear Coffin's appeal. The justices ordered the execution delayed while they considered the argument, but decided in the end that the court had no jurisdiction to overturn Abbott's original decision.

There was one last chance. Gravel sent a written appeal directly to federal Justice Minister Stuart Garson, asking him to order a new trial in light of new evidence. Wilson McGregor, who had testified at the trial that he had seen the barrel of a rifle in the back of Coffin's truck, swore out a new statement claiming that he could not be sure if what he had seen had been, in fact, a rifle barrel. It might simply have been a length of iron bar.

"It could have been a rod of iron. I never saw a hole in the end of this rod of iron, nor did I see the trigger or the stock of any rifle," McGregor swore.

There were also witnesses who could testify about seeing two Americans roaming the Gaspé area in a yellow-plywood Jeep around the time of the murders. Among the witnesses was Alwin Tapp, a Moncton police officer who had been vacationing with his brother Gerald and their wives in the area. He claimed he had run into two Americans dressed in army jackets at the Baker Hotel, who were driving a Jeep. The pair had claimed they were going hunting.

On June 8 or June 9, 1953, Dr. William Wilson and his wife, who were originally from Toronto, were on the ferry that travelled between St. Siméon and Rivière-du-Loup when they saw a yellow Jeep on board. Sitting inside the Jeep were two men who apparently had several guns in their possession.

"They could be in their late 20s or early 30s....They wore American army jackets. They had several types of firearms. They gave us the impression they had quarreled or that they were not enjoying their trip," Wilson said.

Lorne Patterson, a resident of Rivière Madeleine, testified that on June 11, 1953, a pair of Americans driving a Jeep had stopped at his garage, asking if anyone had seen the Lindsey party.

At least half a dozen other witnesses later stated that they had seen two Americans of similar description driving around the area in a Jeep at about the time the murder had taken place.

Garson decided against ordering a new trial, but did ask the Supreme Court for advice in the matter. While Gravel and Coffin greeted the news openly, Maurice Duplessis was not impressed. In a press statement, the premier accused the federal government of meddling in provincial affairs.

"The procedures of the governor-general-in-council... were extraordinary, unusual, unheard of and deeply significant from several points of view."

The court's review, however, would be limited in scope. It could not consider the new evidence the jury had not heard at trial. Both the Crown and Gravel made their arguments before the justices, and, in the end, the defence won some battles. There was some consensus that the Crown should not have been permitted to cross-examine Marion Petrie about her testimony at trial and that the hearsay evidence admitted to the court about the disappearance of Eagle's rifle should not have been allowed. Unfortunately for Coffin, only two of the seven justices voted in favour of a new trial. The remaining five declared in a majority ruling that the conviction be upheld.

The court, however, did not make its decision known immediately. In the meantime, Coffin was immersed in another legal battle. He was trying to get permission from the authorities to marry Petrie for the sole purpose of legitimizing his son, James, in the public eye. But the province kept refusing his request because it feared that if the Supreme Court recommended a new trial and Petrie and Coffin were married, as his wife, Petrie could no longer be forced to testify against him. Québec's Solicitor General Antoine Rivard gave Gravel a private assurance that he would allow the two to marry if the court ruled against commuting Coffin's death sentence.

On February 9, 1956, the Supreme Court announced that it upheld Coffin's conviction. Though Gravel appealed directly to Garson for clemency shortly after the decision was announced, his plea was rebuffed. Even with Coffin's fate sealed, the province still refused to allow him and Petrie to marry.

"I don't understand. I don't understand," Coffin is quoted as saying. "I'm innocent."

At midnight on February 10, Coffin received communion and sang hymns with Anglican Reverend Sam Pollard. Coffin recited the prayer for the dying, kissed his prayer book and stated, "I am not guilty, and may God have mercy on my soul."

The noose was affixed around his neck, and as witnesses, including Matte, watched on, the trap door sprang open and Coffin's body fell through the floor. Fifteen minutes later, he was pronounced dead.

His case, however, never died. Coffin left behind a 48-page living will and testament in which he vigorously denied every single aspect of the Crown's case against him. He never once tried to change the story he had given the police from day one of the investigation.

"I repeat I am innocent of this crime and I feel I was not give a fair trial, chiefly that evidence about the presence of another Jeep and other Americans in the Gaspé District was held back and that evidence of the marks of a Jeep on the road in the vicinity of the camps was also held back," Coffin wrote.

~

Approximately 500 people attended Coffin's funeral at York Centre later that month. In a symbolic gesture that he believed Coffin's innocence, Reverend Pollard ordered Coffin buried in consecrated ground.

It did not take long for the doubts surrounding Coffin's conviction and execution to reach the public. In 1956, John Edward Belliveau, a journalist, published *The Coffin Murder Case*, in which he castigated the entire investigation and conviction of Coffin. Journalist Jacques Hébert, who was later appointed a senator, followed up with three works: an essay entitled "Coffin Was Innocent," a book entitled *I Accuse the Assassins of Coffin* and an updated version of the book, entitled *The Coffin Affair*. *I Accuse* drew on follow-up interviews with many witnesses and included the full text of Coffin's final will and testament, which led to widespread criticism over how the case had been handled.

But the most disturbing revelation came in November 1958, when the police in Miami, Florida, arrested Francis Gilbert Thompson—35 years old and of the Mohawk nation in St. Régis, Québec—on a charge of vagrancy. Shortly afterwards, Thompson told the police he had assisted in the triple homicide of the Lindsey hunting party in Canada back in 1953.

The Miami police knew little about the case and contacted the QPP to let them know what they had found. The QPP, however, did not respond enthusiastically. In fact, Hébert took it upon himself to travel to Miami and personally interview

Thompson, while the QPP merely gave the Miami Police Department a list of 20 questions to put to Thompson.

According to Thompson, he and a man named Johnny Green had hitchhiked part of the way to the Gaspé, stole a Jeep and drove the rest of the way. They had come across the Lindseys and "a guide," all of whom they killed. They had later drowned the Jeep in the St. Lawrence River.

Thompson was originally co-operative and answered all 20 questions, giving answers close enough to the truth to raise eyebrows in Miami. The QPP responded with an attempt to discredit Thompson, issuing a statement from Thompson's mother that her son was actually confined to a sanatorium at the time of the murders. A phone call to the Brockville institution revealed that although Thompson had been a patient there, he had been admitted and released before the murders had occurred.

Within three days, Thompson's tune had changed completely. He denied everything, claiming he just wanted to get back to Canada. He was later transferred into the custody of the RCMP and then released without further investigation. He was last seen in Toronto.

In his book *The Coffin Affair*, Hébert states that during the time between Thompson's arrest and his denials, a notary named J. Conrad Moreau, who had close ties to the Union Nationale party, disappeared from Québec and apparently went to Miami. Hébert, however, stops short of accusing Moreau of any wrongdoing, and his claims have never been substantiated.

The pressure to exonerate Coffin continued to build until January 8, 1964, when new Québec Premier Jean Lesage ordered the creation of a Royal Commission on the Coffin Affair. Judge Roger Brossard was appointed as its head. The commission sat from March 2 until July 3 for a total of 415 hours, examining 436 exhibits and interviewing more than 200 witnesses. The 693-page report produced at the end upheld Coffin's conviction and execution.

On February 10, 2006, 50 years to the day of Coffin's execution, several generation of his family converged on his gravesite to proclaim his innocence. Seven months later, after having fallen out of touch with his family for more than 20 years, Coffin's son, James, reunited with other members of his family.

That same year, journalist Lew Stoddard announced he was beginning a thorough review of the entire Coffin affair. He regularly posts updates to wilbertcoffin.com.

Chapter Six

Steven Truscott

Golderich, Ontario
September 29, 1959

When the fever was breaking
I was sweat soaked and frail
I dreamed I was
Steven Truscott a child in jail
— *Truscott* by Blue Rodeo

N o one had once seen the young boy cry. He had spent the last two weeks sitting in the prisoner's box in the Goderich courtroom, listening as men almost three times his age argued either for or against him. To the spectators and witnesses seated inside the chamber, it seemed as though the Crown and the defence were arguing over the 14-year-old's soul.

In a sense, they were arguing over the boy's destiny because the charge he faced was the most serious under the Criminal Code. It was hard to believe, especially in 1959, that a teenage boy was capable of being more than a nuisance. It was more difficult to believe that anyone his age could be capable of rape. It defied reason further still that he could be guilty of murder.

But that's what the Crown had spent 15 days trying to prove. Before the eyes and ears of 12 local men, Crown prosecutor Glen Hays had called a steady stream of witnesses, all of whom seemed to have some incriminating evidence to share. And yet as each witness spoke, the teenaged boy had watched on, seemingly undisturbed by the sickening allegations the Crown was trying to prove.

Frank Donnelly, the boy's defence lawyer, had put up a spirited fight against a mountain of evidence and testimony. He had humiliated the Crown's key forensic witness, cast suspicion upon the testimonies of the officers who had investigated the case and put forward witnesses of his own whose stories seemed to many more concrete and believable than what the Crown was trying to prove. He had hoped to win over the 12 men in the jury booth, who would decide the boy's fate.

The jury had finally left, but their absence hadn't lasted long. In the span of two hours they had been called back to the courtroom four times, once at their own request and the remainder after Donnelly objected to the directions of trial judge Ronald Ferguson. The somber ambience of the courtroom now held all the seriousness of a kindergarten class as the judge and the defence seemed to play musical chairs with the jury. No

sooner would the group receive their new instructions and clari-
fications and disappear than the door would open again, and
they would file back in to take their seats. Ferguson had grown
visibly more irritated each time and Donnelly increasingly
cowed by the judge's growing fury.

The sun was long gone by the time the jury filed in for
the final time. While most families were at home in their beds,
the crowd at the courthouse was too preoccupied to think of
sleep. With his parents watching, the boy took his seat again
and waited silently while everyone else around him vibrated ner-
vously. His fate now hung on the lips of a jury foreman.

"Gentlemen of the jury, have you reached a verdict?"
Ferguson asked.

"Yes, my Lord," the foreman replied.

"Do you find the prisoner at bar guilty or not guilty?"

"We find the defendant guilty as charged, with a plea for
mercy."

There were gasps of shock, sighs of relief and sobs of sor-
row. The boy's face seemed to turn white in shock. No sooner
had the foreman spoken than Ferguson turned to the boy,
charged with violently raping and murdering Lynne Harper
only three months before, and laid down his sentence.

"Steven Murray Truscott, I have no alternative but to
pass the following sentence upon you. The jury have found you
guilty after a fair trial. The sentence of this court upon you is

that you be taken from here to the place from whence you came and there be kept in close confinement until Tuesday, the eighth day of December, 1959, and upon that day and date, you be taken to the place of execution and that you there be hanged by the neck until you are dead.

"And may the Lord have mercy upon your soul."

And then, for the first time since the ordeal began, the boy's eyes welled with tears.

Despite the sentence, Truscott would not die. And neither would his case.

~

Lynne Harper was missing.

The word spread through the air force town of Clinton, Ontario, like a brush fire, consuming the imaginations of its residents.

The 12-year-old girl had, according to her parents, left her home on the night of June 9, 1959, in a sour mood. It had been sweltering, the mercury tickling the 30°C mark, and the young girl had wanted to go swimming at the base pool. Neither her father, Leslie, an officer with the Royal Canadian Air Force (RCAF), or her mother, Shirley, had the time to take her. Instead the girl had a quiet supper—her family had already eaten—and then shot out the door in the hopes of getting a pass to swim at the base alone. Unsuccessful, Lynne returned home, and after washing the dishes, left again without telling anyone where she was going.

Lynne's curfew had always been 9:00, but when the hour rolled around, she was nowhere to be found. Leslie and Shirley at first shrugged off Lynne's tardiness, but they grew increasingly frightened as the minutes ticked by. Finally concerned, Leslie left his home to go searching for his daughter.

The Harpers weren't yet sure how worried they needed to be. In fact, they wondered early on if their sometimes headstrong daughter might not have made her way to nearby Highway 8 to thumb a ride to her grandmother's home in Port Stanley. They didn't know for certain, though, and Leslie decided to alert the guards at the base.

He contacted the base at around 11:30 PM and spoke with the non-commissioned officer in charge of guard detail, explaining that Lynne was missing. A squad made a quick trip to the base pool but didn't find anyone there. The corporal on duty contacted the nearby Exeter detachment of the Ontario Provincial Police (OPP) to pass on the information to the officers patrolling the area. A car stopped by the Harper home, where an officer borrowed a photograph of Lynne. Her description was then broadcast to 10 other counties.

But as the sun rose the next morning, there was still no word from Lynne or any sign of her. Still patrolling the streets looking for his daughter, Leslie stopped by the home of an enlisted man, Dan Truscott, to see if anyone there had seen her.

Dan's 14-year-old son, Steven, seated at the breakfast table, spoke up. According to the boy, he had been out on his bicycle around 7:25 the previous evening when he ran into Lynne at the school. She had asked him for a ride down to the highway and he had obliged, doubling her on his handlebars. He said he had left her at the intersection of the highway and the county road north of town and then started biking back. He had stopped at the bridge spanning the nearby river and looked back, where he saw her get into a car that he thought resembled a 1959 Chevrolet.

Steven would tell the story hundreds of times over the next 48 years, but the details would never change. When he arrived at school later that morning, an OPP officer pulled him out of class and asked him to repeat his story. The police questioned him again when he returned home for lunch later that day, when he gave a more detailed description of the recently redesigned Chevy. He told them that the vehicle had whitewall tires and lots of chrome and that he had seen something yellow on the back of the car.

The police returned again later that evening and this time took Steven and his mother, Doris, on a ride down the county road to the highway. Little did Steven know that the OPP were already starting to wonder about his story. Earlier that day, an officer had gone down to the bridge and spent some time watching cars drive by. He hadn't been able to make out the licence plate numbers on any of the cars. It shouldn't have mattered because Steven had never told anyone that he actually saw the licence plate numbers on the car, but no one seemed to have remembered that.

The morning of June 11, the OPP again yanked Truscott out of school and questioned him. This time they asked if any of his friends had seen him during the bike ride, and Truscott was pretty sure someone had. After all, he'd ridden his bike over the bridge on a hot day when many of the town's youngsters had been swimming, splashing and chasing turtles in the river. He gave the officer a few names and then went back to class.

By the following afternoon, Truscott's honesty would place him squarely in the sights of the OPP.

⁓

The RCAF guards had originally decided that no search for Harper was necessary, but they mustered the troops early on the afternoon of June 11 to begin scouring the area for her. Teams briefed on Harper's appearance were dispatched all around the area, looking for any sign of the missing girl.

Later that afternoon, word came back that the search had been tragically successful.

One search team had headed north along the county road towards the highway and meandered onto a small lane locally referred to as the tractor trail. Farmer Brian Lawson, a friend of Truscott's, used the trail to get the tractors from his property to his nearby field. The area around the trail was covered in trees, and kids referred to it as Lawson's bush.

It was in Lawson's bush, just off the tractor trail, that the team had stumbled upon a horrific discovery. Lying face up in the grass, covered in three maple branches, was Harper's half-naked body. The team passed the word on to the police, who called for a pathologist.

The scene Dr. John Penistan arrived at later that afternoon was, by later accounts, so puzzling that it should have given any investigator pause. The body, which showed dramatic signs of decomposition and insect activity, was dressed in only a bloodstained undershirt, but there was only a miniscule amount of blood found in the soil at the scene. The vegetation and earth around Harper's body were hardly disturbed, but no one seemed to notice.

The cause of death, according Penistan, was obvious. Harper's turquoise blouse had been tied under her left jaw in a ligature, apparently strangling her to death. The rest of her clothes were found nearby, her socks rolled up neatly, the zipper on her shorts fastened. Her panties were found several feet away.

Three nearby maple trees showed evidence that branches had been ripped from their trunks, which corresponded to the three branches found draped over Harper's body. A fourth tree sported a branch that someone had obviously tried to break off, but hadn't been able to. A search of the ground area also turned up a comb, some tissues, two pop bottles and a half-eaten hot dog, possibly signs of a picnic.

One of the air force officers who had found Harper's body claimed he had spotted a footprint in the dirt just beside the girl's left foot. A forensic officer photographed the mark, but later determined it to be a scuff mark without any identifiable characteristics. Other marks found near the scene included tire tracks from a bicycle and possibly a car.

After spending an hour collecting evidence, Penistan ordered Harper's body to be removed from the site and taken to the local funeral home for autopsy.

The results of the examination of the body would raise questions even 48 years later.

～

Considering that much of the Crown's case would later be based on Harper's stomach contents, it seemed strange that no one could say for sure what she had eaten for dinner before she died.

According to Julian Sher's book *Until You Are Dead: Steven Truscott's Long Ride into History*, Lynne's mother had served her turkey, dressing and peas. There was also bologna and ham in the fridge if the girl had wanted, and for dessert there had been three kinds of cake, including upside-down pineapple cake. Shirley later admitted that no one actually saw Lynne eat; the family had already finished their dinner when Lynne came home.

Working in the funeral home, Penistan began his examination, originally pegging Harper's time of death at approximately 9:00 PM on June 9. The cause of death was ruled as strangulation by ligature, given the blouse found knotted around the girl's neck. Penistan also noted scratch marks on Harper's arms, feet and legs. He recorded bruising to the vaginal area but couldn't identify any semen—only "a considerable number of ill-defined, diffusely stained bodies."

In the company of base doctor David Hall Brooks, Penistan emptied Harper's stomach contents into a jar and examined them by holding them up to the light. He noted "one pint of poorly masticated, only slightly digested food including peas, onions and corn." It was the most extensive analysis Penistan would perform on the stomach contents.

Yet based on that information, Penistan made a claim that would shape the entire case against Truscott. Although Penistan originally estimated Harper's time of death as approximately 9:00 PM, he later refined that time to an exact 30-minute period between 7:15 and 7:45 on the evening of June 9.

Back in 1959, before forensic practices evolved to the higher standard we now know, estimates of time of death using stomach contents were considered iffy at best. Any number of factors can either quicken or slow digestion, including intense fear or a heavy meal. The standard rule of thumb that the stomach empties within two hours of eating is not hard and fast, but Penistan made his findings on that basis. If, as the Harpers later testified, Lynne ate at approximately 5:45 PM on the day she disappeared, and her stomach was not yet empty when she was killed, then she must have died before 7:45 PM.

Despite the time estimate, the first police warning to hit the streets seemed to indicate that there might be some credence to Truscott's earlier statements about what had happened when he had dropped Harper off at the highway. A dispatch to OPP units in the area warned officers to keep an eye out for any 1959 Chevrolets with yellow licence plates. Officers were also asked to observe the occupants for scratches to the face, neck, hands and arms. Analysis had revealed skin tissue underneath Harper's fingernails, indicating that she had most likely put up a fight.

But that wasn't consistent with the evidence found at the body site—there were no signs of a struggle. It also didn't fit with the boy who would become the one and only suspect in the murder case.

~

Inspector Harold Graham arrived in Clinton on the evening of June 11, 1959, to investigate Harper's death. The investigation lasted less than a day.

It was Graham who issued the original alert warning officers to be on the lookout for anyone with scratches on their persons. That same release contained an estimated time of death for Harper of 9:00 PM. Yet by the next morning, though he would later maintain that Truscott was "not a strong suspect originally," Graham was already marshalling his forces to start pecking away at the unsuspecting 14-year-old.

It was difficult for anyone to contemplate that Truscott was capable of such a crime. He was a gifted athlete who played hockey and football. He wasn't an honours student, but he wasn't a troublemaker either. Truscott was well known in town by most of its residents and liked by most of the local kids.

But his story, in Graham's mind, was just too coincidental. Now that Penistan had refined his estimate of the time Harper died, it seemed as though Truscott was the only person who could possibly have killed her. By Truscott's own admission, he was the last person to have seen her.

On the morning of June 12, Graham pulled Truscott out of class for yet another interview. The boy repeated his story, but denied it when asked if he had any interest—romantic or otherwise—in Harper. He gave Graham the names of four boys who had been swimming at the river when he had passed by on his bicycle with Harper, including Dougie Oates and Arnold "Butch" George.

Graham followed up with the boys. Oates had a self-confessed interest in the wildlife that inhabited the area and told Graham he had been hunting for turtles with a friend near the bridge when he looked up and saw Truscott and Harper ride by. "Lynne was on [the] crossbar," he said. Oates' story corroborated that of Gord Logan, another boy who was down by the river on

June 9 and had told the police on June 11 that he had seen Truscott and Harper cross the bridge.

Both were stories Graham hadn't really wanted to hear. If witnesses could place Truscott with Harper on the bridge, which was located in between the highway and the tractor trail, then Truscott's story might be true.

George's story, however, was never nailed down to the satisfaction of the police, the Crown or the defence. According to the boy, he had also seen Truscott and Harper together, biking over the bridge towards the highway. George's story, however, would change repeatedly, over not only the next few days, but the next few months.

The police did have one suspect whose testimony gave them pause. A young girl by the name of Jocelyne Gaudet had spoken twice with the police and told them she had arranged to meet Truscott in Lawson's bush to look at some calves that had recently been born. Gaudet said she had headed down the county road to the bush at around 6:30 PM on June 9 and waited, but Truscott had never come. She also told the police she had had a funny feeling while she was walking up the tractor trail, but never explained exactly what that funny feeling had been.

∾

By the afternoon of June 12, Graham was convinced he had the killer in his sights.

Harper's stomach contents had arrived at the Attorney General's laboratory in Toronto earlier in the day. According to Graham, his conviction was verified later that afternoon when biologist Elgin Brown stated that a preliminary examination revealed that Harper had eaten her last meal within two hours of her death. In Graham's mind, that meant Truscott was the murderer.

A police car was dispatched to pick up Truscott from the Lawson farm, where he had been doing some chores, and take him to the Goderich detachment. Although it was standard practice at the time, Graham decided not to inform Truscott's parents that he had brought the boy in for questioning and instead spent the next 90 minutes trying to coax a confession out of Truscott. The 14-year-old stuck to his original story and refused to incriminate himself. Graham ordered Truscott back to the guardhouse at the air force base near Clinton.

Dan Truscott, having learned from Lawson that the police had picked up his son, made his way to the air force base where he found the police questioning Steven. At the prompting of an OPP officer whom he believed to be a friend, Dan consented to have two doctors examine Steven. One was Brooks, and the other was a local family doctor named John Addison.

While both men were competent doctors, neither had any forensic specialty, especially when it came to charges of murder and rape. Yet the results of their examination would further fuel the investigation against Truscott. The pair asked him to remove his clothes, and they documented a series of scrapes and cuts, not uncommon in a boy of 14. None of the scratches were deemed fresh or recent.

As they progressed through their examination, the two doctors took a look at Truscott's genitals and found what Addison would later describe as "a very sore penis."

Both doctors documented one sore about the size of a quarter in diameter on each side of the shaft of the boy's penis. Their report stated that the sores resembled "a brush burn with serum oozing from each of those large sores on the side."

They asked Truscott what had happened. He was naturally shy and stated that his penis had been bothering him for four or five weeks, but that he hadn't said anything about it. The doctors asked him if he'd tried having sex with a girl or if he'd snagged his penis in something, both of which Truscott denied. He did, after repeated questioning, admit quietly that he had masturbated the week before. No one, with the exception of his father, believed his story.

As the doctors were examining Truscott, officers with the OPP executed a search warrant on the Truscott home. The team took from the house a pillowcase, two sheets, a wool blanket, a pair of red pyjama bottoms, a pair of brown shoes, a shirt, some underwear and a pair of red jeans found hanging on the clothesline outside. The police noted that the jeans were the only item of clothing hanging on the line at the time of their search.

No one could shake Truscott's story. Despite their efforts, neither Graham nor Addison was able to elicit a confession from the juvenile suspect. In Graham's eyes, though, it didn't matter. The sores on Truscott's penis, he believed, were indicative of recent sexual activity and proof that Truscott could have raped and murdered Harper.

At approximately 3:00 AM on June 13, the OPP transferred Truscott back to Goderich and officially charged him with first-degree murder in the slaying of Lynne Harper.

~

Harper's body was laid to rest on June 13, the same day Truscott made his first appearance in court. After a brief debate, an Ontario magistrate ruled that the boy, though only 14, would stand trial as an adult, not as a juvenile, for the good of the community. The difference between the potential sentences in each case was blatant: a conviction as juvenile would mean a brief prison term, but a conviction as an adult would mean a date with the hangman.

The hearing concluded without mention of granting Truscott bail. He was shipped to the Huron County jail, where officers arrived shortly afterwards to seize his underwear, which, by his own admission, he had been wearing for the last four days.

Over the next few days, the OPP spent their time doing what they hadn't done in the first few days following the discovery of Harper's body—investigating. They interviewed approximately 20 people over the weekend after Truscott's arrest, going so far as to set up a makeshift headquarters in the school gymnasium. One by one, the local kids trotted in and shared their stories with the police.

One of those kids was Gaudet, the girl who said she was supposed to meet Truscott in Lawson's bush on the night Harper had disappeared. Her story, however, had changed. She now told the police that Truscott had initially asked her to tell no one about their planned rendezvous. The pair was supposed to meet at "the right-hand side of the county road where the bush began." She even said she had asked Truscott to wear something that would stand out so she could spot him. In the opinion of the OPP, which was later put forward as an argument by the Crown, Gaudet may have been Truscott's original target, and he had settled on Harper when he didn't find Gaudet.

But there were problems with some of the times the witnesses were giving the police. Truscott maintained that he had met Harper around 7:25 PM on June 9 at the school and biked her down to the highway. According to Gaudet, she had left around 6:30 and then run into Arnold George and Phillip Burns on the county road near the river. When both boys denied seeing Truscott that night, she had gone down to the river and then over to Lawson's farm, where she had spent 90 minutes chatting before heading back home.

There were several problems with Gaudet's story. For starters, no one had seen her down at the bridge that evening.

Secondly, both George and Burns stated they had run into Gaudet, but it had been closer to 7:15. Lastly, the police never bothered checking Gaudet's story with Lawson, who would later state that the girl had visited for substantially less than 90 minutes.

Gaudet's testimony about timing was just the beginning of a problem both the defence and the Crown would later spend a great deal of time arguing about. The Brownie guides who had seen Harper approach Truscott outside the school told the police that the pair had taken off around 7:10, even though Truscott claimed it had been closer to 7:25. Neither was really sure of the time, though. There were two other boys—Richard Gellatly and Phillip Burns—whom one woman said she saw leave the bridge at approximately the same time, around 7:00. Gellatly had ridden his bike to the bridge, while Burns had walked. Gellatly told the police that he had passed Truscott and Harper heading the other way. Burns said he hadn't seen the pair. Because Gellatly and Burns had been on the same road at the same time but travelling at different speeds, the police assumed that Truscott and Harper had veered off into the bush after passing Gellatly, but before Burns had reached the turnoff from the county road to the bush. Officers in the community also heard a rumour that George was telling people he had seen Truscott enter the bush with Harper, even though he had reported nothing of the sort earlier on.

The police also did some experimenting of their own that they felt bolstered their case. They parked a 1959 Chevrolet at the intersection of the country road and the highway and took photos, trying to determine if Truscott could have read a licence plate from the bridge. They finally concluded that he couldn't have.

But on June 19, 10 days after Harper's body had been found, a young girl turned up an important piece of evidence the police had somehow missed. She found on a barbed-wire fence an RCAF locket that Harper had been known to wear. The locket, found intact, was located well away from the spot the police believed Truscott and Harper had entered the bush, but the police had searched the area thoroughly when they found Harper's body and hadn't found the locket.

Graham was willing to look only so far in his investigation. He never bothered investigating known sex offenders in the area, even though a CBC documentary later turned up the name of an air force officer with a drinking problem who had a history of trying to lure young girls into his car. Graham settled on what he had to date, which turned out to be a raft of questionable forensic evidence, dubious eyewitness testimony and a suspect who refused to cry.

~

Frank Donnelly had been appointed as a judge of the Superior Court in Ontario, but when the Truscotts approached him about representing their son, he delayed starting his new position in order to take the case. He had no idea that he would become inexorably linked with wrongful convictions. His son

James would later preside over the murder trial of another man wrongfully convicted of murder, Guy Paul Morin.

Donnelly tried to appeal the decision to try Truscott as an adult rather than a juvenile, but he was refused. The preliminary inquiry, which began July 13 in the court of Magistrate Dudley Holmes, heard from 31 witnesses over the course of two days as Crown prosecutor Glen Hays tried to prove to the judge that there was enough evidence to warrant sending the case to trial. Donnelly's position as Truscott's defence lawyer was a difficult one. Disclosure laws requiring the Crown to turn over to the defence team all relevant evidence in their case against the accused were virtually non-existent in 1959, meaning that Donnelly would have to prepare the bulk of his client's defence based on what he heard during the preliminary inquiry. Also, the Crown was not required to tender all of the evidence it presented at the hearing later at trial. The inquiry was essentially a proving ground where Hays could test-drive some of his witnesses and evidence and later decide what was going to work and what wasn't.

There were some obvious holes in the Crown's case right from the start. A forensics officer testified to the court that the so-called shoeprint found at the scene had been too scuffed to identify, but when Penistan took the stand, he told Holmes that the print belonged to someone approximately 5'7" or 5'8" in height, about the same as Truscott. Penistan also testified that he had, using the progression of rigor mortis and the maggot population in the body, narrowed the time of death down to sometime between 7:00 AM on June 9 and 7:00 AM on June 10. Harper's stomach contents, he told the court, had further honed his estimate to between 7:15 and 7:45 PM.

Truscott's jeans, which the Crown had been hoping would yield evidence, bore little fruit. The stains found on the knees were nothing more than grass, experts said. The issue of bicycle tire marks at the scene also came up at the inquiry. A set had been photographed in the area around Harper's body, but a forensics officer testified that the depth of the marks indicated they had been made sometime when the ground was wet. It had not rained near Clinton for several weeks.

While some of the evidence was dubious, there was enough of it, Magistrate Holmes ruled, to warrant sending the case to trial. He ordered Truscott bound over for a jury trial, which would begin on September 16, barely three months after Harper's body had been found.

~

The case was sensational. A 14-year-old boy, charged with capital murder? The chance that he could actually be hanged for raping and killing a playmate? It had all the elements of a gripping story, but when the trial began in Goderich, there were few reporters in attendance.

There were plenty of spectators, however. The Truscotts were plainly visible in the courtroom, there to support their son.

The family had moved out of Clinton to be closer to Steven, who had been awaiting trial in custody at the Huron County jail. Dan had been transferred to a base near Ottawa and was commuting on weekends.

Ninety local residents received jury notices and attended the Goderich courthouse for jury selection. In the end, 12 jurors, all men, were empanelled to hear the case of Regina versus Steven Truscott.

Judge Ronald Ferguson, a no-nonsense kind of judge, had been selected to preside over the courtroom proceedings. While the jury was responsible for determining whether or not Truscott was guilty, it was Ferguson's job to make sure both counsels followed the rules, that witnesses were properly sworn and that evidence was correctly presented based on both statute and common law.

The age of some of the witnesses was of concern to the judge. With some as young as 11 scheduled to testify, it was up to Ferguson whether or not these witnesses could be properly sworn. In order to be sworn under oath, a witness had to have an understanding of truth versus a lie and the knowledge that telling a lie was "sinful" and could bring about negative consequences. In fact, several of the child witnesses who testified at Truscott's trial were not sworn because Ferguson ruled they couldn't be.

In his opening argument, Hays laid the case out plainly for the jury. Based on strong circumstantial evidence, including the time of Harper's death as determined by her stomach contents, Gaudet's testimony about her secret meeting with Truscott and police research that proved Truscott could not have read a car's licence plate from the bridge, the Crown believed that Truscott was guilty of murder.

"You will be shown pictures taken from the bridge he was supposed to have seen this from," Hays told the jury. "You will be the judges of what can or cannot be seen."

After calling the forensic officer who first processed the scene, Hays called Penistan, the first pathologist to examine Harper's stomach contents, to the stand. The doctor rambled through his already established evidence—that based on an analysis of her stomach contents, he had determined that Harper had died between 7:15 and 7:45 PM on June 9 as a result of strangulation by ligature. He repeated his remark from the preliminary hearing that the injury to Harper's vagina had been the result of a "blind, violent thrust," without offering any substantiation for his conclusion.

Penistan also told the court that Harper's stomach had contained some vegetables, as well as some traces of turkey and ham. When Donnelly asked why Penistan had mentioned only ham at the preliminary, the pathologist checked his notes.

"I must say, my notes say there was no meat. There was no obvious meat," Penistan was forced to admit to the court.

The Crown suffered another setback the next day when Ferguson ruled that Graham could not testify about Truscott's statement on the night of his arrest. According to Ferguson, the police had not properly warned their suspect, which made Truscott's statement inadmissible. Hays didn't even bother examining the top investigator in front of the jury, while Donnelly asked only about whether Graham knew if it had rained in the area at the time of the murder.

As if school was in session inside the courtroom, a long succession of children and adolescents marched up to the stand to give their testimonies. First came Gaudet, who told her story about the secret rendezvous with Truscott that had never come to pass. Lawson, the tallest witness of the day, followed and testified that while Gaudet had stopped by the farm on June 9, she had stayed for only about 10 minutes, not the 90 minutes she had claimed in her statement.

George's testimony presented a challenge for the Crown because it was always changing. His story had a few components to it. He told the court that he had been on the county road the evening of June 9 but hadn't seen Harper or Truscott. He also said that during a later conversation, Truscott had hinted that the police might try to interview George. George testified that he told Truscott he would tell the police he had seen Truscott at the river.

"He said that the police were going to go down to my place to check up, so I agreed that I would tell them I had seen

Steve," George told the court. The problem was, George hadn't mentioned this particular piece of testimony to the police until after Harper's body had been found, at which point he'd already been interviewed once. Donnelly seized on it.

"And you didn't study your story too well, that is the reason you account for the difference. What is the reason why you tell a different story here today?"

George didn't have a chance to answer before the judge cut him off.

Tom Gillette had another incriminating story. One day shortly after Harper's body had been discovered, he, Truscott and George were talking, and it sounded to Gillette as though Truscott was threatening George to keep his story straight.

Several other boys who had been playing baseball near the school took the stand. They testified that they had seen Truscott return to town sometime before 8:00 PM after having given Harper a ride to the highway.

"How did Steve appear to you when you saw him?" Donnelly asked John Carew on cross-examination.

"Well, he appeared the same as he was any other time," Carew responded.

"Were there any visible marks on him that you noticed?

"No," Carew replied.

"Was there any sign of blood on him?"

"No," Carew responded again.

This line of questioning was indicative of the defence Donnelly was preparing. Several people had seen Truscott when he returned to town. Everyone said he hadn't been breathing heavily or acting suspicious, frightened or nervous, and he had not appeared to have been injured. His clothing had been free of blood. If he had killed Harper, he most likely would have had some sort of scratches on his face or hands from Harper trying to defend herself. Unless he was a psychopath, he would have appeared fidgety and scared. His appearance and behaviour would have been out of character, and those around him would have noticed. Even his parents, who had seen Truscott when he returned home to babysit his siblings, stated that they had seen nothing wrong with their son when he had arrived.

Donnelly was after another piece of evidence he wanted excluded that had to do with the medical exam Addison and Brooks had conducted on Truscott.

The jury was excused as Addison took the stand. Donnelly wanted to argue two points: First, the whole physical examination should be tossed as evidence because Dan Truscott would not have consented to it if he hadn't been encouraged to do so by his friend, who had been an OPP officer. Second, Addison—a doctor, not a police officer—had interrogated Steven at the air force base guardhouse after the exam.

"Did you give any warning to the boy before you asked him questions?" Ferguson asked. "Did you say to him: now what you say to me may be used in evidence?"

"Your Honour, I was examining him as a family practitioner," Addison replied.

"I don't care about your practice!"

"No, I didn't tell him it would be used against him one way or the other," Addison admitted.

He told court that he had asked if Truscott had taken Harper into the bush, if he had killed her and if he wanted to tell Addison about it. Ferguson was furious.

"Every possible sort of inducement, everything to my mind contrary to the rule of the taking of statements took place between Dr. Addison and the boy. Under no circumstances would any court admit that statement in evidence against this accused boy, and I will exclude it."

The ruling meant that, while Addison could still describe the physical exam he and Brooks had performed, he could not utter a word about the private conversation he'd had afterwards with Truscott.

Hays quickly got down to business, asking Addison about the sores on Truscott's penis.

"Is it your opinion that these abrasions could have been caused by a boy [Steven Truscott's] size and age trying to make entry into a girl age 12?"

"Yes, sir. He is sexually developed, the same as any man, and trying to make entry could cause the sores on his penis."

Brooks had two admissions to make up front: that he had seen pieces of meat in Harper's stomach contents and that, though Truscott was generally quite dirty at the time of the examination, his crotch was much cleaner.

He described the lesions on Truscott's penis as "the worst lesions of this nature I have ever seen." He agreed with Addison that the wounds were caused by "a very inexpert attempt to penetration."

Donnelly's ears perked up when he heard Brooks confess that the lesions on Truscott's penis were, in fact, "sixty to eighty hours old." He had testified at the preliminary inquiry that they were likely two to five days old. The change made it appear more likely that Truscott could have raped and killed Harper.

Brooks went on to explain that he had burned and cut himself accidentally in the months since the exam and had based his new estimates on the time it took for his own wounds to heal.

Donnelly wasn't through with the witness. He asked Brooks about a telephone call he had placed the next day to the doctor at the jailhouse in Goderich. Brooks admitted he had called to ask if Truscott was circumcised. Apparently Brooks' examination had been so thorough, it had just slipped his mind.

Biologist Elgin Brown took the stand next. It was his cursory examination of Harper's stomach contents at the lab in Toronto shortly after the autopsy that had clinched the case against Truscott in Graham's mind.

Brown was there to talk about underwear—specifically, the pair of underpants Truscott been wearing that had been seized while he was in jail. The underwear, which hadn't been washed for several days, Brown said, contained some blood and semen. He testified under cross-examination that it was unlikely that the semen dated back to the day of Harper's death because any semen from that day would have been destroyed within hours by the bacteria in Truscott's crotch.

Brown had also found no blood on any of the clothes Truscott had been wearing the day Harper went missing. He testified that they had found blood underneath Harper's fingernails, but it had already been established that Truscott had not been scratched that day.

Donnelly had evidence supporting the theory that Harper had been killed elsewhere. He pointed out to the court that a swatch of the girl's blouse, the same one found tied around her neck, was missing and hadn't been recovered. No one was able to account for it.

Over nine days of the trial, the Crown called a total of 59 witnesses and tendered 76 pieces of evidence. Hays was hoping it would be enough to prove his case

~

Donnelly's first witness was, of all people, a meteorologist. Joseph Calvert, a meteorological instructor from the base at Clinton, took the stand and testified that the last time any rain had fallen in the area was on June 1, 10 days before Harper's body and the bicycle tire marks had been found. Donnelly was trying to prove that because of their depth, the tire marks had been made shortly after June 1, not on the day Harper died.

Berkely Brown, an expert in internal medicine and the digestive system, took the stand next to try to refute the claims Penistan had made based on Harper's stomach contents. Brown told the jury that fixing time by digestion "must be done with extreme caution" because of the number of variables that can interfere with the stomach's digestive process.

He also tackled the issue of the sores on Truscott's penis. He had served in the military during wartime and had examined thousands of penises. He told the court that it was highly unlikely the sores on Truscott's penis could have been caused by intercourse, however rough it might have been.

"It is interesting that the penis is rarely injured in rape, to begin with," Brown said, explaining that any injury would be to the glans, or head, of the penis, not to the shaft. The vaginal wall, he argued, is soft and therefore unlikely to cause any kind of injury.

Doris Truscott took the stand next to try to explain why, of the clothes she had washed on June 10, Steven's red jeans had been the only article hanging on her clothesline.

"The band at the top was still damp and the pocket lining was wet and I just threw them over the line," she explained.

She also said she had washed the jeans in hot water, meaning that any blood that might have been on them would have been set into the pants. Earlier testimony had established that there was no blood found on the jeans, only grass stains.

Next came Dougie Oates, the nature hunter, who had been catching turtles down by the bridge on June 9. He had told the police that he had seen Truscott and Harper ride by on the bridge between 7:00 and 7:30 PM.

"What did Lynne do?" Donnelly asked.

"She smiled," Oates replied.

"What did Steve do?

"I don't think he noticed me because he just kept riding down."

Hays knew Oates was trouble for his case and tried to attack the child's story. But the 11-year-old defended himself with a piping voice.

"Other witnesses have told us of seeing Steven down there by himself at 6:30 PM, Douglas," Hays said. "Is there a chance that that is what you saw?"

"No, it isn't, sir."

"Did you simply add Lynne through things you heard after?"

"No, I saw him and Lynne."

Oates' older brother Allan also testified, saying that on the day in question, he had left home to head down to the river on his bike. On his way there, he had seen Truscott standing on the bridge. He estimated the time had been between 7:30 and 8:00 PM.

Donnelly's final witness was Gord Logan, who had also been down by the river, alternating fishing and swimming, when he looked up and saw both Truscott and Harper ride by on Truscott's bike. Five minutes later, he said, he had seen Truscott return across the bridge alone.

The Crown now had a chance to call rebuttal witnesses. Hays first called a Crown secretary named Marjorie Gardner, who had taken notes on Dougie Oates' first interview. According to Gardner's notes, Dougie had told the police he had seen Truscott and Harper ride by "a half hour either way of seven."

Dougie insisted that the testimony was wrong, that he had seen the pair closer to 7:30.

Paul Desjardine, who had also been down by the river, told the court that he saw Dougie and a friend leave the bridge at 6:30. Under Donnelly's cross, however, Paul stated that he could be mistaken, saying, "I don't remember too well."

After striking out with one of the kids' mothers, who said she hadn't noticed anyone in particular by the river, Hays set his sights on Logan by calling OPP Constable Donald Trumbley to the stand. Trumbley had taken Logan down to the bridge on July 6 to test his eyesight. Trumbley himself acknowledged that he hadn't been able to make out the features of anyone on the bridge at the time. Suddenly, Judge Ferguson interrupted.

"Do you think you could recognize a man in a suit of clothes, if he had on a red shirt or white shirt, at two hundred yards?"

"Yes, I believe so."

Donnelly faired even better in his cross.

"Was there any test made of Gord Logan to see whether he could recognize anyone on the bridge?" the lawyer asked.

"No, sir," Trumbley admitted.

No one expected Donnelly to be so brazen as to put a 14-year-old accused killer on the stand, and he did not. Trumbley was the last witness called in the two-week trial. It was now September 28, and all that was left was the lawyers' final arguments, the jury's charge and the verdict.

～

Throughout both the preliminary hearing and trial, Truscott sat quietly in his chair, watching the proceedings. Even as the Crown assassinated his character, he refused to cry or blush. He sat there like a rock, appraising the situation before him, watching with a clinical eye.

In the Crown's opinion, it was a killer's display of a total lack of remorse.

Donnelly was up first for his final argument, and he focused on the tenets of his defence, the witnesses who had seen Harper with his client at around 7:30 PM and then saw him alone shortly after. He trashed the Crown's forensic evidence, stating that no one with Penistan's training could possibly narrow the time of Harper's death down to a 30-minute window based on her stomach contents. And he argued that the sores on Truscott's penis could not possibly have come from raping Harper.

"I am confident that after careful attention that you can come to only one conclusion and one finding, and that is a verdict of not guilty for this boy. It is with confidence that I leave the fate of this boy in your hands."

Hays' final argument came next. He laid out the timing from the Crown's point of view, claiming that Truscott had had time to rape and kill Harper and make it back to Clinton by the time his friends saw him. He rallied the jury to support Penistan's theories, underscored the Crown's theory that Harper had been killed exactly where she'd been found and reminded them of Gaudet, whom he asked to stand up in the courtroom.

He told the jury that "but for the grace of God [Jocelyne] could have been the victim of the sexual predator sitting in the prisoner's box."

In Hays' mind, the answer was clear: Truscott was guilty. He wanted the jury to believe so too.

"I submit, gentlemen, that, on all of the evidence, there is only one conclusion that you can reasonably come to…and that is that the accused committed this crime."

Next came the charge to the jury, which turned out to be devastating for the defence.

Ferguson told the jury to ignore Gaudet's secret-date evidence because it was unreliable. He also warned them not to get too obsessed about the actual timing of the events in question.

Ferguson did wonder how Gellatly had seen Truscott and Harper while he was on his way home from the river and Burns, who had left at the same time on foot, had not. "Do you think Steve and Lynne went into the woods at that interval? That is entirely for you to say. It is not for me to say."

Then came the shock of the trial. While discussing which witnesses saw what at the bridge, Ferguson took the uncharacteristic step of introducing his own theory of the crime into the trial—that Truscott had doubled Harper across the bridge and then brought her back as well.

"Is it possible the accused brought her back?" Ferguson asked. "You'll ask yourselves, if this boy is guilty, why has he shown such calmness and apathy?"

It is rare for a judge to introduce his or her own theory of the crime, but it does happen, and Donnelly was incensed. No sooner had the judge completed his charge and the jury filed out than Donnelly rose to object to Ferguson's charge on a number of points. First, he pointed out, Burns' testimony was uncorroborated and unsworn. He then offered his most important objection—that the judge's theory could wrongfully sway the jury towards a conviction.

"There is no evidence to indicate that he brought her back. Any evidence would be that he didn't bring her back."

"Well, she was back. This is where they may draw the inference he brought her back because she was back," Ferguson responded.

Donnelly tiptoed along the line of proper courtroom decorum when he also suggested that a jury listening to the charge might have gotten the impression that a guilty verdict was required based on the evidence.

"What's wrong with that?" Ferguson replied.

The jury was recalled and Ferguson put a new charge to them, containing the objections the defence had brought forward. The jury filed out and was called back in one more time because Ferguson had neglected to mention the defence's theory on Truscott's penis lesions. The judge agreed and explained that the defence was arguing the injuries were caused by masturbation or "any roughness, any knothole or any mechanical device or anything of that kind."

At 8:38 PM the jury finally filed out.

At 10:05 they returned.

They didn't have a verdict yet. They had a simple question. They wanted to hear the evidence "of Lynne Harper and Steven Truscott being seen together on the bridge on the night of June 9."

Ferguson reviewed the evidence with them, again resurrecting his own theory about Truscott bringing Harper back from the highway, and then sent them off. Donnelly stood to object.

"I submit there is no evidence to warrant them finding that."

After a brief argument, Ferguson called the jury back to the courtroom and explained that there was no evidence that Truscott had brought Harper back from the highway. But as the jury prepared to leave again, Ferguson threw in another caveat—that the testimonies of the prosecution's witnesses were perhaps more reliable than those of the defence's witnesses. Donnelly again objected after the jury filed out. A red-faced Ferguson promptly called them back in and clarified his point.

The jury was gone for only 10 minutes. When they returned the next time, they had their verdict ready.

Steven Truscott was guilty. The jury, however, pleaded for mercy.

Ferguson wasted no time. When Truscott declined to say anything in response to the verdict, the judge announced the sentence. On December 8, corrections officials would take Truscott to the gallows, where he would be hanged.

"And may the Lord have mercy upon your soul."

For the first during the entire trial, Truscott's eyes filled with tears.

Donnelly tried to reassure Doris and Dan Truscott that the state would never hang a 14-year-old, but everyone was too shocked by the words.

With a crowd of 200 waiting outside, an officer rushed Steven out the back door to a waiting car that would take him back to jail. The tears were gone.

"I just wasn't brought up that way," Truscott told journalist Sher. "It's not the air force way."

～

On November 20, 1959, the federal cabinet ordered a delay of Truscott's execution to allow his new lawyer, John O'Driscoll, to appeal Truscott's sentence to the Ontario Court of Appeal.

Donnelly had taken his appointment as a judge, and O'Driscoll was coming into the case with a fresh perspective. On January 12, 1960, he appeared before the justices of the Court of Appeal to argue for a new trial. O'Driscoll was limited in what he could bring forward because practices at the time prevented the defence from tendering any new evidence in an appeal. The focus of his argument, therefore, was limited to any possible errors of law that had occurred during Truscott's trial.

O'Driscoll argued that Ferguson had not sufficiently explained the defence theories to the jury and that it had been inappropriate for him to put forward his own ideas about what might or might not have happened. Ferguson also erred because he didn't tell the jury that they could also acquit Truscott of the charge.

The justices disagreed. On January 20, two days after Truscott turned 15, his appeal was dismissed.

Truscott did win one significant battle outside the court-room. The day after his appeal was denied, the federal cabinet met again and voted to commute his death sentence. The convicted teenager would no longer hang; instead, he would spend the rest of his life behind bars. In February, the Supreme Court of Canada refused to hear Truscott's appeal of his conviction. As per its usual practice, the court gave no reason for the refusal.

With all of his legal avenues exhausted, Truscott resigned himself somewhat to a life behind bars. He spent the first three years of his sentence with dozens of other juvenile delinquents at the Ontario Training School for Boys outside Guelph. His days were spent working in a woodworking or machine shop and his evenings, in school. In between, a steady succession of psychiatrists paid him clinical visits, wanting to study the mind of a so-called child killer and possibly elicit some sort of confession. While some later stated that Truscott obviously suffered from some sort of psychosis, the teenager never budged from his story.

He was still making news, even though he was locked behind bars. George Wadrope, the provincial minister for reform institutions, visited the School for Boys and spent several minutes chatting with Truscott. He later caused a firestorm of public criticism when he publicly stated that he felt "a great deal of doubt" about Truscott's guilt.

For a boy who everyone thought was going to be a troublemaker, Truscott distinguished himself by his good behaviour during the three years he spent at the juvenile institution. He was never once written up for any sort of in-custody charge. He listened to his guards, did everything he was asked and never picked fights or caused any other kind of trouble. Eventually, Truscott's mild-mannered behaviour earned him the trust and respect of the school's top brass. When he turned 18, the staff even lobbied the government to allow Truscott to remain at the school, but sentencing guidelines mandated that once he legally became an adult, Truscott had to serve the remainder of his sentence in an adult facility. In 1963, the boy, now considered a man, was transferred to the Collins Bay penitentiary in Kingston.

Truscott continued to win over everyone around him. Although the nature of his crime—the rape and murder of a child—put him on the lowest end of the prison society totem pole, he became quite popular and managed to convince most of the people around him that he was innocent. He continued his good behaviour inside, working in the machine shop and doing as he was told. He never once tried to escape.

The psychiatrists followed him to the penitentiary and continued to try to dig into the recesses of his mind. One in particular, Dr. George Scott, seemed determine to break Truscott. He subjected the boy to repeated examinations, including several using drugs such as sodium pentothal—a so-called truth serum—and even LSD, a hallucinogenic agent the United States government was testing on unwitting suspects in their own country and in Canada as a possible means to mind control. Regardless of the agent used, Truscott still refused to change his story.

In 1966, a book hit the streets that, for the first time, put Truscott's entire conviction into question. Written by Isabel LeBourdais, *The Trial of Steven Truscott* was printed in England because there were no Canadian publishers willing to take on the issue of Truscott's conviction.

LeBourdais took special issue with the physical evidence found at the scene of the crime, explaining to the public for the first time the police's curious findings, many of which had never been made public before. She pointed out that while Harper's undershirt had been soaked in blood, there was only one wound found on her entire body—a puncture to her left shoulder—and investigators had found less than tablespoon of blood on the ground around her body. LeBourdais also argued that though Harper had been found covered in branches ripped from nearby trees, Truscott hadn't been tall or strong enough to rip those branches off.

The book was a robust criticism of the case against Truscott and generated a tide of empathy for the now 21-year-old man. In response to the growing public backlash, the federal cabinet ordered a Supreme Court review of Truscott's conviction and asked the court to decide if, based on the rules of law and the evidence, its finding would have been different.

For the first time, Truscott would finally get the chance to tell his story.

~

The Supreme Court of Canada does not hear trials. It hears arguments from lawyers on points of law in controversial cases and rules accordingly. But Truscott's review was the second in 10 years that would involve the court calling witnesses and acting, in effect, as trial judges. Almost a decade before, the justices of the high court had reviewed the death sentence of Wilbert Coffin. Now they would review the case against Truscott.

The court opened session on October 5, 1966. The hearing quickly descended into a battle of experts as pathologists for both the Crown and defence argued over Penistan's original findings regarding Harper's stomach contents and her time of death. Strangely enough, Penistan himself never took the stand.

Arthur Martin was now responsible for Truscott's defence. He brought forward two other pathologists—Dr. Charles Sutherland Petty from Maryland and Dr. Francis Edward Camps from London, England—who criticized Penistan's use of stomach contents to determine time of death. They also introduced a new element into the defence—photos of Harper's body showed that some parts of her left-hand side were pale in colour, what the experts referred to as blanching. Petty, an assistant medical examiner, testified that this blanching could indicate that Harper had been placed on her left side for a period of time after death. Everyone knew that the girl had been found lying on her back.

Truscott took the stand on October 6, but his performance turned out to be lacking. For a man who had been waiting for seven years to tell his side of the story, his memory proved to be less than adequate as he struggled to remember dates and times. He did tell his original story to the court, that on June 9, 1959, he had met Harper at around 7:30 PM near the school, given her a ride on his bicycle and left her at the highway. He said Harper had been mad at her father for not letting her go swimming.

He also told the justices he had been too embarrassed to tell anyone about the sores on his penis, which he said he'd noticed about six weeks before his examination. Several doctors would later testify that they had treated Truscott for a skin condition called dermatitis, which could explain the sores.

"Did you kill Ms. Harper," Martin asked Truscott at the end of his testimony.

"No, I didn't," Truscott replied.

The justices of the court, however, were unwilling to overturn the conviction. On May 6, 1967, in an 8–1 decision, the court ruled that they saw no reason to overturn the verdict. In their ruling, the court accepted that Harper had likely been dead by 7:50 PM. They also accepted the testimony of Burns, Gaudet and George that the trio should have seen Truscott and Harper on the road. The majority said they found it impossible to believe that a boy could have such visibly painful sores on his penis for six weeks and not mention it to anyone.

The ruling was final. There were no other avenues for Truscott to explore. He went back to jail and watched as his parents, having suffered almost eight years of incredible stress, finally separated. He spent his Christmases alone, his days working hard and his evenings in university classes at nearby Queen's, having been permitted to study there. Finally, on October 21, 1969, 10 years after his original sentence, Truscott was granted parole. He was discharged into the care of United Church chaplain and parole supervisor Malcolm Stienburg and ordered to live under an assumed name. After a few stops in different communities, Truscott eventually made his way west to Vancouver to live with his grandfather.

Before he made the trip, Truscott was introduced to a young woman named Marlene, who had been following his case for years and was one of his supporters through Isabel LeBourdais, who was still fighting to prove his innocence. When Truscott moved to Vancouver, Marlene also made the trip. The pair started spending more and more time together, and a relationship blossomed. Shortly afterwards, they married privately in a ceremony devoid of friends or family, gifts or pictures. They moved back to Guelph to be close to Marlene's family, where Truscott found work as a millwright. They had three children and continued to live a quiet life. Truscott never denied who he was if asked but never went out of his way to make himself publicly known. He wanted to protect his family.

That all changed in 2000. The family had been approached several years prior by the CBC, asking if the station could do a review of Truscott's case on its flagship documentary series, *The Fifth Estate*. At Marlene's prompting and with the support of his children, Truscott agreed. The documentary team succeeded in acquiring police reports, autopsy reports and trial transcripts that gave them the evidence they needed to openly question Truscott's conviction. On March 29, 2000, *His Word Against History: The Steven Truscott Story* made the boy from Clinton a household name again as approximately 1.4 million viewers tuned in to watch the documentary. A flood of emails, letters and postcards supporting Truscott arrived at both the CBC and Truscott's home.

Two months later, Truscott was ready to take his fight back to the courts. He retained James Lockyer of the Association in Defence of the Wrongfully Convicted to file an appeal to the justice minister of Canada under section 690 of the Criminal Code. The section allowed the minister to review any conviction and decide if any action should be taken to correct a possible miscarriage of justice.

The government responded in 2001 by appointing retired judge Fred Kaufman, who had already made a name for himself by overseeing the Royal Commission that investigated the wrongful conviction of Guy Paul Morin, to prepare a report on whether or not a miscarriage of justice might have occurred. Kaufman reviewed the case and filed his report in the spring of 2004, stating that a miscarriage of justice likely had occurred. On October 28, 2004, Justice Minister Irwin Cotler announced that he was asking the Ontario Court of Appeal to review Truscott's conviction.

On April 6, 2006, Harper's body was exhumed in the hopes that investigators might find some trace of DNA that could be used to definitively confirm or exonerate Truscott as the killer. Unfortunately, the pathologists who examined her remains, which were now 47 years old, found nothing of value.

The court convened on June 19, 2006, and heard evidence up until July 7, 2006. Much like the Supreme Court hearing from 40 years ago, the arguments turned into a duel of forensic experts, focusing not just on stomach contents, but also on maggot growth.

Because the life cycle of maggots, whose eggs are laid in human flesh within hours of death, is predictable, their age can be helpful in determining time of death. Two defence pathologists testified that in their opinion, the life cycle of the maggots found on Harper's body indicated that she had died sometime between 11:00 AM on June 10 and 8:00 AM the following morning. The Crown called forward its own expert, who testified that Penistan's original evaluation of time of death was likely true.

The Court of Appeal also heard some other disturbing evidence. According to one Crown witness, former OPP officer Harry Seyeau, neither Inspector Graham nor any other members of the team investigating Harper's death had bothered investigating other known sex offenders in the area. Farmer Brian Lawson told the court two interesting details. He said he had seen a strange car parked near the fence on his land on the evening of June 9. He also testified for the first time that, on the day before he was scheduled to testify at Truscott's first trial, Jocelyne Gaudet had approached him and tried to convince him to change his testimony to reflect hers.

Lawson wasn't the first witness to publicly question Gaudet. A nursing student, Sandra Stolzman, who had later shared a residence with Gaudet, told the court that on one occasion, Gaudet had admitted to several girls that she had lied under oath when she gave testimony at Truscott's trial.

The court adjourned on July 7, 2006, and reconvened on January 31, 2007, with one new change. For the first time in its history, the Court of Appeal allowed its proceedings to be filmed. What followed were nine days of oral arguments as lawyers from both the defence and the Crown put the finishing touches on their cases. The CBC broadcast the sessions live during the day.

On February 10, the justices retired to consider their decision, which, as of the writing of this book, is expected sometime in August. They are required to give both the Crown and the defence three days' notice once they have reached a decision.

On the morning of August 28, 2007, the Court of Appeal released its decision:

"The court unanimously holds that the conviction of Mr. Truscott was a miscarriage of justice and must be quashed....The court thus orders that Mr. Truscott should stand acquitted of the murder of Lynne Harper."

In a 300-page written decision, the justices agreed that fresh evidence brought before the court during the review, particularly pertaining to time of death, could have affected the jury's original decision had it been available to them. A jury could have reasonably doubted Harper's time of death as proposed by the Crown.

In deciding the appropriate remedy, the justices had three options: enter an acquittal on Truscott's behalf, order a new trial or order a new trial and enter a stay of proceedings. Because a new trial would be "a practical impossibility," that Truscott and his family had lived with the burden of the original verdict for nearly 50 years and that the justices believed a jury was more likely to acquit Truscott at a new trial than convict him, the Court held that quashing the verdict and acquitting him of the crime was the best remedy.

Unfortunately for Truscott, the justices stopped short of declaring him innocent of Harper's murder: "The court is not satisfied that the appellant has been able to demonstrate his factual innocence."

Ontario's Attorney General Michael Bryant informed the press shortly after the decision was released that the Crown did not plan to appeal and that he had appointed former Ontario Court of Appeal Justice Sydney Robbins to advise the government on how to compensate Truscott.

"On behalf of the government, I am truly sorry," Bryant said. "It is a decision that will not be appealed by the Crown…it is over."

In a press conference held after the ruling was released, Truscott told reporters the decision was the end of a lifelong fight to clear his name.

"For 48 years, I was considered guilty," he remembers. "I knew myself, and my family knows that I never was. So just to hear the decision…I never in my wildest dreams expected in my lifetime for this to come true. So it is a dream come true."

Notes on Sources

Anderson, Barrie and Dawn Anderson. *Manufacturing Guilt: Wrongful Convictions in Canada*. Halifax: Fernwood Publishing, 1998.

Belliveau, John Edward. *The Coffin Murder Case*. Toronto: Kingswood House, 1956.

Harris, Michael. *Justice Denied: The Law versus Donald Marshall*. Toronto: MacMillan of Canada, 1986.

Hébert, Jacques. *The Coffin Affair*. Toronto: General Paperbacks, 1982.

————. *I Accuse the Assassins of Coffin*. Montreal: Benjamin News, 1964.

Karp, Carl and Cecil Rosner. *When Justice Fails: The David Milgaard Story*. Toronto: McClelland and Stewart, 1998.

Kaufman, Fred. *Royal Commission on Proceedings Involving Guy Paul Morin*. Ontario Ministry of the Attorney General, 1998.

LeBourdais, Isabel. *The Trial of Steven Truscott*. Toronto: McClelland and Stewart, 1966.

Makin, Kirk. *Redrum the Innocent*. Toronto: Penguin Books, 1992.

Malloy, Ronald. *Guilty Till Proven Innocent: The Thomas Sophonow Story*. Toronto: R.M. Publications, 1987.

Milgaard, Joyce and Peter Edwards. *A Mother's Story: The Fight to Free My Son David*. Toronto: Doubleday, 1999.

Sher, Julian. *"Until You Are Dead": Steven Truscott's Long Ride into History*. Toronto: Random House, 2001.

Trent, Bill. *Who Killed Lynne Harper?* Montreal: Optimum Publishing, 1979.

WEB SOURCES

Canadian Press. "Donald Marshall Jr. sent for further medical assessment." *CTV.ca*, February 2, 2006. http://www.ctv.ca/servlet/ArticleNews/story/CTVNews/20060202/donald_marshall_060202/20060202/.

CBC News Online. "CBC News In Depth: David Milgaard." *CBC.ca*, December 2006. http://www.cbc.ca/news/background/milgaard/.

———. "CBC News In Depth: Steven Truscott." *CBC.ca*, January 22, 2007. http://www.cbc.ca/news/background/truscott/.

————. "CBC News In Depth: Wrongfully Convicted." *CBC.ca*, February 15, 2007. http://www.cbc.ca/news/background/wrongfullyconvicted/.

Injusticebusters. *Thomas Sophonow: His Fight for Compensation.* http://injusticebusters.com/2003/Sophonow.htm.

Lett, Dan. "Ex-prosecutor's cases questioned." *Winnipeg Free Press Live*, June 21, 2007. http://www.winnipegfreepress.com/local/story/3992576p-4607934c.html.

Manitoba Justice. *The Inquiry Regarding Thomas Sophonow.* http://www.gov.mb.ca/justice/publications/sophonow/index.html?/.

Sher, Julian. "The Wrong Man in the Right Place." *The Walrus*, February 2006. http://www.walrusmagazine.com/print/2006.02-field-notes-the-wrong-man-in-the-right-place/.

Stanley, Wendall M. *Wilbertcoffin.com: Our Quest for Justice.* http://wilbertcoffin.com.

Peter Boer

In his position as assistant editor and as a reporter for the *St. Albert Gazette*, Peter Boer has covered everything from city council meetings to crime. His on-the-job experience, much of which has been spent in courtrooms throughout the Capital region in Edmonton, as well as his background in psychology, has led him to a fascination with the bigger picture of crime in Canada. He has examined both its roots and the effects of crime on people on a local and national scale. Boer has penned seven other non-fiction titles, and his successful storytelling style draws the reader into the lives of the people he portrays.

Check out more True Crime from

QUAGMIRE
PRESS

MISSING!
The Disappeared, Lost or Abducted in Canada
by Lisa Wojna

The people in this book have one thing in common—they all vanished, many without a trace. Some of the cases featured in the heart-wrenching stories in this book are:

- Nicole Hoar, planning a surprise visit to her sister in Smithers, disappeared while hitchhiking along BC's infamous Highway of Tears
- Sex-trade workers had been disappearing from Vancouver's downtown Eastside for 20 years before law enforcement began investigating Robert William Pickton
- The families of Ontario's Lost Boys still wonder what became of them after the six took a late-night cruise on Lake Ontario
- Jessie Foster's family uncovered hints of human trafficking when the young woman vanished after moving from Kamloops to Las Vegas to join her new boyfriend
- Despite national and international publicity, no one has stepped forward to identify a young man dubbed Mr. Nobody after a brutal beating put him in a Toronto hospital

$18.95 • Softcover • 5.25" X 8.25" • 256 pages
ISBN-10: 0-978340-90-6 • ISBN-13: 978-0-978340-90-2